The Newly Qualified
Secondary Teacher's

in S

David Fulton Publishers
London

David Fulton Publishers Ltd
Ormond House, 26–27 Boswell Street, London WC1N 3JZ

www.fultonpublishers.co.uk

First published in Great Britain by David Fulton Publishers 2000
Reprinted 2001

British Library Cataloguing in Publication Data

A catalogue record for this book is available from the British Library

ISBN 1–85346–682–4

Typeset by FiSH Books, London WC1
Printed in Great Britain by The Cromwell Press, Trowbridge, Wilts.

Contents

Acknowledgements

I am indebted to several people for their advice and assistance in writing this book:

Christopher Arnold (Walsall LEA Educational Psychology Service), Rod Blaine (Sneyd Community School) and Heather McLachlan (Shenley Court School, Birmingham) wrote or contributed to chapters. Their names are given in the headings to the respective chapters. Chris Arnold's chapter is drawn from a very successful classroom and behaviour management course for NQTs devised and run by Walsall's Educational Psychology Service.

Dr Bob Preston (Wolverhampton University School of Education) read and helpfully commented on each of the chapters. Syd Houghton-Hill and David Brettell (Walsall LEA inspectorate) supported the production last year of a prototype version of this book designed for use by induction coordinators and tutors.

There are various short extracts in this volume from educational books, journals and in-service training materials that I have found very useful when running the induction programme at my school over the last few years. I wish to record my gratitude to their publishers for permission to include the quotations.

Introduction

The DfEE's new induction arrangements

Under the terms of the 1998 Teaching and Higher Education Act, all newly qualified teachers who are awarded Qualified Teacher Status (QTS) now have to complete a three-term induction period. Induction is a concept that represents this first year in teaching as a necessary bridge between the pre-service education you received on your university or college training course and the more self-directed role of the experienced teacher. The induction provision you receive in your first school will seek to smooth your transition from student to teacher and make it as developmental as possible. Its formative nature cannot be over-emphasised in terms of helping you fit into the classroom and your school, specifically, and the profession at large.

Crucial to the process will be the support, monitoring and guidance you receive from your induction tutor as part of the induction programme. He/she will act as a mentor, which is a concept that features in the language of education and the wider world of the professions, social services and business. Mentoring's origin in Greek mythology points to a figure who is a wise and trusted adviser and friend. There is a variety of mentoring functions that your induction tutor could take on – training, developing, counselling, negotiating, supervising, assessing, sharing, trusting, sponsoring, guiding, etc. Inevitably, you will find he/she makes an individual interpretation of the role, since few of us can do everything! Nevertheless, you should find that a dynamic and reciprocal professional relationship develops between you.

The success of your induction year will also be helped by your new school's commitment to its success. Undoubtedly, you will be welcome in your first appointment – but not because you are cheaper to employ! Rather, the attraction will be the freshness and vitality that you are expected to bring to your department and the staff in general. Beyond this, you will find a good induction school is one where opportunities are available to *all* staff to enhance their professionalism. It will be a place where a lively and critical approach to teaching and learning processes is encouraged. There will be strong professional relationships. The school's aims and policies will be shared and put into practice. Finally, there is likely to be a style of leadership and management at senior and departmental levels that thrives on discussion, collaboration and teamwork.

The DfEE's induction arrangements, as laid down in Circular 5/99, focus on a judicious combination of entitlements and expectations for newly qualified teachers. The Government regards them as a key part of its overall strategy for raising educational standards and performance. The main provisions are summarised below.

Roles and responsibilities of key personnel involved in induction

Head teachers – They hold joint overall responsibility with the LEAs for the supervision and training of NQTs. They must:

- ensure an appropriate induction programme is set up;
- recommend to the LEA whether an NQT has satisfactorily met the requirements for the induction year;
- keep the governors informed of induction arrangements and assessment meetings.

LEAs – They have responsibility with heads for NQT supervision and training, and must decide if NQTs have met the Induction Standards. They must ensure heads and governors know about and meet their statutory responsibilities for NQT support and assessment. This role as the 'appropriate body' should be addressed in the LEA's Education Development Plan.

Induction tutors – This role covers the work of induction coordinators and subject/ classroom mentors. They must be:

- fully aware of induction requirements;
- in possession of the necessary skills and knowledge;
- able to make rigorous and fair judgements;
- capable of providing effective support.

NQTs – There are a number of entitlements for NQTs included in Circular 5/99. These include a job description that does not make unreasonable demands and provision of preliminary information relating to:

- timetable
- the induction tutor
- induction meetings
- assessment
- sickness procedure
- pay arrangements
- health and safety
- equal opportunities
- school policies
- employment contract
- duties rota
- details of the school's management

In return, NQTs must:

- use their Career Entry Profiles for target setting their professional development during induction;
- take part in the school's monitoring, support and assessment programme;
- familiarise themselves with the Induction Standards and use them in monitoring their own work;
- develop increasing responsibility for their professional development.

Governors – They should ensure the school is capable of providing the necessary monitoring, support and assessment.

NQT training and development needs during induction

The induction programme – The programme for NQTs should:

- offer monitoring and support tailored to their individual strengths and needs as identified in their Career Entry Profiles;
- build on their knowledge, skills and achievements within the framework of the QTS and Induction Standards;
- involve the setting of short, medium and long-term objectives based on individual and school priorities;
- regularly review progress via formative and summative assessment.

This means NQTs should be actively involved in planning their induction programme. All documentation relating to observations and review meetings should be open and accessible. Any concerns NQTs have about their induction programme should be raised, first, with the school and, then, a named LEA contact.

Monitoring and support – The programme for NQTs should involve:

- support from a designated tutor;
- lesson observation and review;
- professional review of progress;
- observation of experienced teachers;
- other targeted development activities.

The induction tutor should monitor and support on a day-to-day basis, although the roles of support and assessment could be given to *two* people. Activities and their outcomes should be documented.

Lesson observations should occur at least half-termly and focus on particular aspects of teaching based on agreed criteria identified in the Standards and Career Entry Profile (CEP). Observations should have a follow-up discussion, with documented targets for action. Observations may be carried out by staff other than the induction tutor, by Advanced Skills Teachers or by university staff.

Half-termly meetings should be held to review progress, based on observations and other evidence. The CEP is an appropriate form of record. Opportunities should be provided for observing experienced colleagues in the NQT's school or in another where there is acknowledged good practice. Time released by the reduced teaching load should be used for induction activities.

Other components in the programme of support could include:

- information on the school, post and induction arrangements;
- information on rights and responsibilities, induction tutors and assessment;
- participation in the school's general INSET programme;
- details of school policies, e.g. behaviour management, child protection and health and safety;
- opportunities to work with the school SENCO;
- attendance at training organised by external agencies.

The LEA – Its responsibilities include:

- maintaining a data base of NQTs;
- identifying a named contact;
- collecting in all summative assessment forms;
- informing NQTs, head teachers, the DfEE and General Teaching Council of decisions about the successful completion of induction.

Assessment and quality assurance during induction

Assessment arrangements – Guidance is provided on:

- summative assessment meetings;
- evidence used for assessing progress;
- reporting procedures.

There should be three, termly formal assessment meetings between the NQT and head teacher or induction coordinator, focusing on these questions in turn:

1. Is the NQT consistently meeting QTS Standards and beginning to meet Induction Standards?

2. What progress is being made to meeting the Induction Standards?

3. Has the NQT met the requirements for satisfactory completion of induction and what objectives are set for the second year of teaching?

Documentary evidence to inform these meetings should be drawn from at least two observations and two progress review meetings, supported by:

- pupils' assessment data;
- details of liaison with colleagues and parents;
- lesson plans and evaluations;
- evidence of the NQT's self-assessment and professional development.

Written records must be detailed in cases of unsatisfactory progress. All records should be available to NQTs and the LEA. All records must be retained until any appeal process is complete. Circular 5/99 provides templates for the documentation that should be completed at each summative assessment meeting and then sent to the LEA. It includes space for the NQT to make a comment.

Where a small minority of NQTs make unsatisfactory progress, they should be given early warning and concerns should also be communicated to the LEA. It should not be left till the summative assessment meeting. Head teachers should observe NQTs at risk and put in writing the consequences of failure. The reports on NQTs making poor progress should give details of:

- identified weaknesses;
- agreed objectives;
- planned support;
- evidence on which the judgement is based.

LEAs have an obligation to ensure:

- assessments of NQTs are accurate;
- weaknesses have been correctly identified;
- appropriate objectives for improvement have been set;
- a support programme is in place.

Recommendations for passing induction must be made to the LEA within 10 days of completion. The LEA must respond within 20 days. Extensions to the induction period before its completion will be permitted only in situations where there is absence for 30 or more working days or if a request is made by someone on maternity leave.

Where a period of induction is extended (only in exceptional circumstances) or an NQT is deemed to have failed, details must be given of the right to appeal to the Secretary of State (eventually the GTC). NQTs who appeal against failing induction must be dismissed or employed on restricted duties (they cannot teach a class or subject in their own right).

Quality assurance – The LEA has overall responsibility for quality assurance. It must ensure heads and governors are aware of, and carry out, their responsibilities. It must also ensure assessments are fair and support is given to NQTs at risk. This can be done via:

- link inspectors' visits;
- monitoring a sample of schools.

OFSTED inspections will now include induction arrangements.

The purpose and structure of this handbook

This book is intended as a practical guide to the key professional issues that newly qualified teachers in secondary and middle schools are likely to face at different stages of the induction year. It offers a structured diet of ideas, approaches and activities that should prove useful as a continuous source of reference throughout induction. Organised along the lines of an 'open learning' programme, its content is based on training and development resources used at Sneyd Community School and other schools in Walsall over the last five years or so.

Part One comprises eleven chapters of structured support materials covering professional issues commonly featured in secondary schools' induction programmes. Of course, some of the topics will need to be amended or extended to include the particular circumstances found in your new school, e.g. the workings of the pastoral system, use of ICT in the classroom or the mechanics of report writing. It is important to remember, too, the emphasis that will need to be put on your individual needs assessment through use of the Career Entry Profile.

Nevertheless, each chapter is designed to provide you with a variety of accessible insights and activities for use during induction and in collaboration with your induction tutor. My intention, when writing this book, has been to draw upon research into identified good practice, so that the content meets your practical and immediate needs. At the same time, there is an attempt to provide a theoretical foundation based on research and literature on the different topics. By doing this, it is hoped you will be better equipped to reflect on the wider, underlying issues. References are cited at the end of each chapter to make it easier for you to consult them.

In Part Two the book goes on to include detailed guidance on lesson observations, review meetings and target setting. There are sections on using the QTS and Induction Standards and the Career Entry Profiles in your support, monitoring and assessment. The final chapter offers guidelines for undertaking a structured exercise in critical self-reflection towards the end of your induction. This would involve you identifying areas of professional interest or concern, and then seeking to devise and implement a strategy for improvement with one class, or even just a group of pupils, over a four or five week period.

Part One

Chapter 1

Getting started in the classroom

For almost all of us at the start of our teaching careers, the first few weeks in front of our classes were challenging, to say the least! They tested our professionalism *and* our personal stamina. This is the time when we were learning to disentangle and get our heads round some of the initial complexities of the process of teaching. Research shows that for most new teachers, the first priority is establishing an orderly classroom atmosphere and a positive pupil relationship. Once that is under your belt, you can afford to let your management tactics become less visible and concentrate on your teaching and learning activities. There is more of an implicit understanding, between pupil and teacher, of what is expected. That is why learning to teach is a *developmental* process.

So this first section examines three issues that should enable new teachers, at the earliest stage of the induction year, to cope more effectively with classroom management:

1. What is involved in being an effective teacher?
2. How can new teachers get to know pupils?
3. How should the classroom be organised?

What is involved in being an effective teacher?

Current thinking recognises that quality of teaching is central to effective education. Schools will always be concerned about issues like curriculum design and structure, efficient systems of management, and ways of measuring attainment and progress. But teaching – and teachers – have rightly come into their own as the most vital components of effective schools. With the home, they are recognised as the decisive factors in pupils' learning. That is why OFSTED places the main force of inspection on the observation of teaching and the extent to which it contributes to successful learning.

In Victorian times, Wragg (1974) informs us, teacher-training institutions were described as 'normal' schools. He says this presupposed agreement over one single, approved method that all novice teachers had to follow. It manifested itself in the 'object lesson' – a set piece that was deemed to have universal application. In *Hard Times*, Charles Dickens refers to 'some 140 schoolmasters [who] had been turned at the same time at the same factory, on the same principles, like so many pianoforte legs'.

There is, perhaps, a hint of this approach today, albeit on a much more sophisticated level, if we bear in mind pointers towards a general prescription of favoured methods like:

- the Teacher Training Agency's Standards for the Award of QTS;
- the DfEE's Induction Standards;
- the OFSTED Chief Inspector's views on 'orthodox' teaching methodology;
- Professor David Reynolds' call (1998) for 'an applied science of teaching'.

The research literature on effective teaching is vast and complex, which is why the tendency in initial teacher training in recent times has been to encourage a variety of approaches. Nevertheless, there *is* a degree of consensus about the generic features of effective teaching. Here are two typical summaries that explore *effective teacher behaviour.*

Pupils achieve more, when a teacher does the following:
- emphasises academic goals
- makes them explicit and expects pupils to be able to master the curriculum
- carefully organises and sequences the curriculum
- clearly explains and illustrates what pupils are to learn
- frequently asks direct and specific questions to monitor pupils' progress and check their understanding
- provides pupils with ample opportunity to practise
- gives prompts and feedback to ensure success
- corrects mistakes and allows pupils to use a skill until it is over-learned or automatic
- reviews regularly and holds pupils accountable for work

(Doyle 1986, p. 95)

Effective teachers:
- are clear about their instructional goals
- are knowledgeable about their content and the strategies for teaching it
- communicate to their pupils what is expected of them – and why
- make expert use of existing teaching materials in order to devote more time to practices that enrich and clarify the content
- are knowledgeable about their pupils, adapting teaching to their needs and anticipating misconceptions in their existing knowledge
- address higher as well as lower level cognitive objectives
- monitor pupils' understanding by offering regular, appropriate feedback
- integrate their teaching with that in other subject areas
- accept responsibility for pupil outcomes
- are thoughtful and reflective about their practice

(Porter and Brophy 1988, pp. 74–85)

A lot has been produced about *effective teaching skills*, too, as part of the Government's standards-raising agenda. The ability to conceptualise and articulate practice in precise, technical language is relatively new – the best teachers have always tended simply to do these things and take them for granted. However, the list on the following page is typical of various research studies and reflects skills consistently noted as being important.

The question of *how best to teach* has tended to focus on two contrasting teaching styles – the 'traditional' didactic and 'progressive' discovery approaches. Researchers have found difficulty in relating particular teaching styles to effective learning outcomes and results. The sheer diversity of teaching situations and contexts probably makes a direct link impossible to establish. They also comprise a false and over-simplified dichotomy. If the truth were known, effective teaching is a sophisticated and multi-layered activity, which is too complex for recipe solutions. Most teachers use a judicious repertoire of approaches and styles suited to the different learning situations they encounter. Twelve years ago, the National Evaluation of TVEI concluded that 'a teacher who mixes his/her methods as appropriate to the topic is doing much as we would commonly ask'.

Effective teaching skills:
- Organisational – *to sort out materials and sources of information*
- Analytical – *to break down complex sources of information*
- Synthesising – *to build ideas into arguments*
- Presentational – *to clarify complex information without harming its integrity*
- Assessing – *to judge the work of pupils so that appropriate feedback can be given*
- Managerial – *to coordinate the dynamics of individuals, groups and classes*
- Evaluative – *to improve teaching continually*

(Mortimore 1994: pp.290-310)

✎ Activity 1.1
This is designed to help you clarify *your* view of what constitutes effective teaching. It is a form of 'personal construct' theory. It allows you to examine your own emerging thinking and constructions by comparing and contrasting them with other individuals.

STEP 1
Think of two teachers who taught you – one in whose lessons you think pupils learned a lot and enjoyed being present, the other the opposite. Then jot down a brief descriptive paragraph about each teacher, with a couple of examples, e.g.

- *patience to explain things, even if you didn't understand first time – I was really frustrated with a Maths problem, so he just sat and did it with me till I understood*
- *unfair in her use of punishments – once kept whole class in because one boy hid someone's PE kit*

STEP 2
Now list some dimensions of teaching that have emerged from Step 1. Try to use phrases that are opposites, e.g.

- *friendly but firm/martinet*
- *keeps pupils on task/loses pupils' attention*
- *enthusiastic and lively/dull and boring*
- *provides lots of learning activities/lessons are chalk-and-talk*
- *provides routines and strategies/disorganised and vague*

STEP 3
Finally, looking at the positive characteristics, identify some specific and practical ways you think you could embody them in your own teaching, e.g.

- *correcting pupil misbehaviour in a calmly assertive manner*
- *regular checks during a written exercise on progress made with questions*
- *inject pace and vitality into reading a passage of prose*
- *provide choice of variety of means of recording a piece of work*
- *ground rules established for classroom entry and handing out books*

(adapted from Wragg 1993, pp. 5–8)

How can new teachers get to know pupils?

More often than not, the classes NQTs face at the start of the induction year are already the result of experiences and expectations and formations over which the new teacher has no control. Vlaeminke (1995) makes the point that they are created by:

- structures within the school
- patterns established by other teachers
- influential norms developed through friendships and allegiances within their peer groups.

In addition, they are the products of their individual backgrounds, both genetic and environmental.

Therefore, it is essential for you *to understand the existing dynamics of any class you take over, and the individuals within it.* This will help to avoid expecting them to do some things that they cannot yet do.

> ✎ **Activity 1.2**
> Think of one lively or difficult class you have encountered already, either in your new school or on teaching practice.
> Identify three behavioural norms for the group and then say what your own expectations are/were, e.g.
>
> - *calling out questions/putting hands up and waiting to be told to speak*
> - *chewing gum/emptying mouths into bin on entering the room*
> - *lack of writing equipment/bringing pen, pencil and ruler to every lesson*
> - *illicit movement/asking permission to move from one's place*
>
> How would you/did you seek to *modify* the pupils' norms in favour of these expectations?

While it is important to develop the ability to think 'on the hoof' in response to the various challenges that you will face in the classroom, Vlaeminke also rightly observes that it is not an admission of failure to turn to other people for help. No teacher is alone, so it is crucial that you acquaint yourself with the appropriate colleagues and school procedures right at the start of the induction year.

So *find out about support systems* on a whole-school and departmental basis. You need to know, for example:

- who you should turn to if you find yourself in troublesome circumstances;
- where to find your head of department or a pupil's year head/form tutor;
- what the school/department procedure is for dealing with disruptive pupils.

Thirdly, it is essential to *know what pupils can actually do* if you are to develop a sound knowledge of their abilities and attitudes. When HMI (1988) surveyed new teachers in schools, they focused on two key aspects of lesson planning and preparation:

- is it clear what the purpose of the lesson is?
- does the lesson take adequate account of the learners' various needs?

In Kyriacou's view (1991), the first question addresses the issue that educational objectives and outcomes should be clearly spelt out. The second concerns how far these objectives take heed of the range and type of pupils' abilities, their previous learning and attainment, and their progress towards future attainment. Keeping a careful note of reading ages, National Curriculum levels and SEN statements are three practical ways of putting your knowledge of what pupils are able to do on a sure footing.

Although seasoned teachers will draw on their years of experience to form a judgement in their minds of the course a lesson should take, careful planning is necessary for teachers at *all* stages of their career. It is particularly important for NQTs, as it will enable you to recognise, and cater for, the variety of skills and abilities you are likely to encounter. Kyriacou reminds us that sensitivity to pupils' needs is one of the most important skills involved in effective teaching. Creating learning opportunities that make it possible to find something to celebrate in each child's performance will boost their self-esteem and make them more willing partners in the learning process. That is why it is essential for you to learn to plan, deliver and evaluate lessons that present realistic and achievable learning outcomes for different pupils.

✎ Activity 1.3

Think about a recent lesson you have taught and review it in the light of the following questions:

- What did the pupils already have to know, understand or be able to do?
- How was their interest aroused or maintained?
- Could any information be presented in alternative ways?
- Were tasks broken down into small steps to guide pupils through their work?
- Were pupils given any strategies to help them to operate on a cognitive level, or were they simply presented with materials?
- Looking at any pupils' mistakes, can you guess why they were made and suggest how they could be avoided in the future?

How should the classroom be organised?

It is vital that newly qualified teachers quickly establish classroom routines that every pupil must follow. They will comprise a synthesis of the school's expectations, the pupils' conduct in other lessons, and your own values and approaches. Classrooms run according to transparent and shared routines have a greater prospect of improving children's learning, motivation and attitude.

It is a fact that your first few lessons will determine, to a large extent, the quality of classroom interaction for the rest of the year. First impressions *are* important. Four actions that will help you to establish a positive working climate are:

- knowing pupils' names;
- establishing 'ground rules' for pupil conduct;
- achieving a controlled entrance and exit to the classroom;
- classroom appearance and seating arrangements.

Learning pupils' names as quickly as possible is the first step for any teacher in building a relationship with a class. Children need to feel they are valued as individuals, so learning their names and then using them frequently gives you a start, especially if a word or two of praise is added. It amounts to basic courtesy, as well as a useful aid in helping to manage youngsters effectively. It is all too easy to become familiar with the names of just a few able children or the 'likely lads' in the back row!

Pupils take teachers more seriously when they are addressed by name, rather than anonymously or by being lumped together, e.g. 'you, boy!' or 'those girls on the table by the door'. It can be awkward to let a pupil see that you still don't know his name after half a term! It also provides a means of reinforcing messages about particular tasks, such as moving furniture or picking up litter. You will need to find your own ways of learning children's names. These could include:

- seating plans;
- name-cards on desks;
- asking pupils to put their hands up when calling a register or returning work.

The large majority of youngsters will happily collaborate with a set of classroom rules, so long as their justification is apparent. Therefore, NQTs should immediately *establish ground rules for behaviour* that they expect in the classroom. Capel *et al.* (1997) stress the importance of classroom rules being 'positive, logical and relevant to the situation'. They need to be clearly defined and expressed, and then applied equably. Some may take a while to establish. Positive rules are those that stress what *can* be done, rather than what can't. They highlight approved, rather than poor, behaviour. They establish goals, rather than issue reprimands. And besides asserting positive action, rules need to have a clear and obvious purpose behind them.

Typical examples of teachers' positive and negative responses are shown below (from Capel *et al.* 1997, p. 66):

Positive	Negative
If you put your hand up, I will come and see you.	Don't shout out.
Work quietly.	Don't talk.
Please walk around the room.	Don't run.
How many examples have you done?	Stop turning round

Good behaviour will not occur after one lesson. Ground rules can take weeks to establish, involving tenacity, hard work … and faith! It may well be worth securing the cooperation of a class in drawing up a set of ground rules that are designed to enhance their learning. Displaying the code on walls or in exercise books will help keep it in pupils' minds. So does giving positive reinforcement to those who keep the rules. Some are non-negotiable, in terms of your personal rules about what constitutes acceptable conduct. Others are likely to prove more flexible, as you try them out with particular classes and as pupils, in turn, get to know your expectations. Above all, be consistent in applying rules and expectations.

Wragg (1984) and Capel *et al.* (1997) suggest certain essential areas that ground rules are likely to cover:

- classroom entry and exit;
- settling down at the start of the lesson;
- asking questions or responding to a teacher's questions;
- movement around the classroom;
- health and safety (e.g. conduct in science labs or in using PE equipment);
- respect for property and equipment;
- written presentation in exercise books;
- making a positive effort;
- verbal communication with other pupils and with the teacher;
- accepting the teacher's authority;
- how pupils are seated or grouped;
- not interfering with the work of others;
- punctuality;
- setting and handing in homework.

A more pithy way of looking at rules is the broad classification used by Smith and Laslett (1993):

- 'Get them in' (greeting, seating, starting)
- 'Get them out' (concluding, dismissing)
- 'Get on with it' (content, manner)
- 'Get on with them' (who's who, what's going on)!

✎ Activity 1.4
Ask your induction tutor to arrange for you to undertake half-a-day of lesson observations of more experienced teachers, so that you can see how school rules are applied inside the classroom. You should compare how the teachers interpret and apply the rules with particular classes or individual pupils.

Achieving a *controlled entrance to a classroom* – so that pupils are in the room, settled and working on task – is vital. The same applies to how pupils leave at the end of lessons. Capel *et al.* (1995) argue that a good start will set the right tone, motivate pupils and underline your authority. Also, it establishes a sense of order and a positive climate for how the lesson should then proceed.

Just think, for a moment, about the first two or three minutes of a typical lesson you have taught and reflect on these questions:

- In what way did the children appear at your classroom door?
- Was there any indication that some of them were in a particular frame of mind, e.g. talkative or tired or over-active?
- Did they take long to settle down?
- What steps did you take to get them working on task?
- Did you get them to see how this fitted in with previous work?

✎ Activity 1.5
Run through this list of possibilities for achieving a controlled entrance and start to a lesson. Consider whether each option seems a *good* idea, a *possible* approach, or should be *avoided*.

Pupils:
- enter the room casually as they arrive
- line up outside and wait for the teacher
- file in silently
- have free choice of where to sit
- can move desks and chairs around
- stand by desks until told to sit down
- respond to a 'good morning' greeting
- go through a hands-on-heads routine
- all face the front, even if seated in groups
- remove their coats
- put their bags on the floor
- are not allowed to chew
- are sent out again if necessary
- engage in social chat

Teacher:
- speaks to incoming pupils
- stands at the door
- sorts out books and materials
- tells pupils that wasted time equals time owed
- takes a register

- waits expectantly for silence, however long
- sorts out individual problems
- makes it clear when the teaching part of the lesson begins

(Vlaeminke 1995, pp. 23–4)

It is equally vital for pupils to experience a sense of orderly finish to a lesson. This will help them to adjust from one lesson and prepare for their next, especially if they face six or eight a day. An organised completion and exit could take this form:

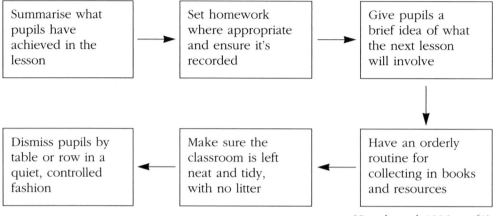

(Capel *et al.* 1995, p. 63)

Finally, a classroom's *appearance and seating arrangements* are two other crucial influences for newly qualified teachers to consider.

Kyriacou (1991) makes some very obvious, but important, points about the impression that the general appearance of a classroom conveys to children. It indicates the care a teacher is prepared to invest in creating an environment conducive to learning. Pupils spend most of the school day in classrooms, so what they see is likely to affect how they regard and value what is taught. Therefore, it should be a place of work, challenge, inspiration and information, as well as offering security and support. In secondary schools, a room should act as a lively and attractive invitation to your subject, e.g. going into a History room should envelop pupils in varied and interesting aspects of the past via posters, drawings and photographs, books, maps, artefacts, etc.

A room full of intriguing words, images and objects will stimulate children from the moment they enter *and* in the pauses which are part of the natural rhythm of lessons. Displays of pupils' work, particularly, will indicate your pride in what they have achieved, as well as motivating those who have produced the material. The way a room is organised is also important. A classroom's layout – such as positioning of desks or provision of special corners – should be functional and appropriate to the style of teaching and learning that NQTs want to take place. However, class sizes or the lack of a permanent teaching base may present constraints.

For 'traditional', whole-class teaching, rows of desks are suitable, although this does restrict opportunities for discussion or contact between pupils. Where active learning methods are favoured – e.g. group work, pupil movement between areas, use of resource boxes or computers, and independent working – seating arrangements will need to take the form of desks positioned together. Pupils can then collaborate easily, access resources or be visited by you ... *but* it does require careful supervision!

What does the attractive and functional classroom look like?

- The room is clean and tidy, occupied only by equipment and materials in current use.
- Wall displays are attractively arranged and are relevant to the current teaching and learning.
- Relevant reading and reference material is available to pupils at all times.
- The layout of furniture gives pupils as much work space as possible and allows for flexibility between individual work, small group work and class teaching.
- There is an adequate supply of all the writing and drawing materials and equipment that the pupils are likely to require.
- The resources for learning currently in use are stored in such a way as to permit quick retrieval.
- When required, there is access to TV, radio, OHP and IT facilities.
- There are clear policies, rules and procedures relating to the shared use of the room by several teachers.
- There is a set of rules governing the use of the room and its facilities by pupils when teaching is not taking place.

(Waterhouse 1990, p. 104)

✎ Activity 1.6

Take a look around your classroom. Identify five aspects that would show anyone walking into it that you are a lively teacher who is doing everything possible to stimulate children to work industriously and enthusiastically.

References

Capel, S., Leask, M. and Turner, T. (1995) *Learning to Teach in the Secondary School*. London: Routledge.

Capel, S., Leask, M. and Turner, T. (1997) *Starting to Teach in the Secondary School*. London: Routledge.

Doyle, W. (1986) 'Research on teaching effects as a resource for improving instruction', in Wideen, M. and Andrews, I. (eds) *Staff Development for School Improvement*, 95. Lewes: Falmer Press.

HMI (1988) *The New Teacher in School*. London: HMSO.

Kyriacou, C. (1991) *Essential Teaching Skills*. London: Simon & Schuster.

Mortimore, P. (1994) 'School effectiveness and the management of effective learning and teaching', *School Effectiveness and School Improvement* **4**(4), 290–310.

Porter, A. and Brophy, J. (1988) 'Synthesis of research on good teaching', *Educational Leadership* **46**, 74–85.

Reynolds, D. (1998) 'Teacher Effectiveness.' Paper presented at the Teacher Training Agency Corporate Plan Launch 1998–2001. London.

Smith, C. and Laslett, R. (1993) *Effective Classroom Management*. London: Routledge.

Vlaeminke, M. (1995) *The Active Mentoring Programme 2. Developing Key Professional Competences*. Cambridge: Pearson Publishing.

Waterhouse, P. (1990) *Classroom Management*. Stafford: Network Educational Press.

Wragg, E. (1974) *Teaching Teaching*. Newton Abbott: David & Charles.

Wragg, E. (1984) *Classroom Teaching Skills*. London: Croom Helm.

Wragg, E. (1993) *Class Management*. London: Routledge.

Chapter 2

Communicating with pupils

Successful teaching and learning depends on the new teacher's effective use of communication skills with his/her pupils. These skills are also an essential part of the repertoire for good classroom management. Most of us *assume* we communicate well. However, when our communication skills are analysed, we may well find scope for polish and improvement.

This chapter explores communication with pupils under two broad headings:

1. Verbal communication
2. Non-verbal communication.

Verbal communication concerns what you say and how you say it. It includes getting pupils' attention, using your voice, talking to pupils in accessible language, explaining, questioning, discussing and listening. Initially, you may think that the words you use are enough. Often, however, you will need *more* than words to say what you mean and so help pupils to do things and understand them. That is why *non-verbal communication* should also be addressed, particularly in terms of how you present yourself to pupils – your appearance, eagerness, confidence and the degree of caring you demonstrate. The non-verbal messages you send out can either support your spoken words or undermine them.

Verbal communication

Securing pupils' attention

Learning cannot take place in the classroom until you have gained pupils' attention at the start of a lesson, or when the class need to listen again after they have been working on a task. So the first thing to do is *act with status*. For instance, standing in front of a class gives you an advantage. It conveys a sense of you being the person in charge. The fact that you are an adult will automatically give you some degree of authority. Make sure you can be seen and heard before you start talking. That means insisting on *silence*! So you need to find some appropriate means of making it clear this is what you want. Once you are talking or issuing instructions, adopt a 'matter-of-fact' *tone of voice* to indicate to pupils that their attention or compliance is expected without question. Link it to eye contact and body posture.

Use of voice

The way you use your voice is vital to classroom communication. It *is* possible to vary how it comes across to listeners in order to add impact and feeling to your words.

People often respond to *how* something is said, rather than *what* is said. You need only listen or watch an experienced politician or TV presenter to note how they use their voices in varied, interesting and encouraging ways.

Capel *et al.* (1995) stress the importance of volume, projection, pitch and speed. Raising or lowering the *volume* is the first step, although it is advisable to keep shouting to a minimum. Noisy, hectoring teachers breed a similar response in their classes! By contrast, a calm, quiet but audible voice level creates a serious and trusting atmosphere. More effective than roaring is developing the *projection* of your voice. This will ensure words leave the mouth confidently and precisely, and be heard further away. Adjusting the *pitch* of your voice also helps to avoid flat and monotonous presentation. Usually, deep voices come across as authoritative and self-assured, especially if they wish to command attention. So to add gravity to what is being taught or said, the pitch should be lowered. However, to add an exciting, lively or humorous touch, it may be appropriate to raise the pitch. Changing the *speed* of what you say can be useful. Measured pauses can suggest confidence, rather than hesitation, while rapid delivery creates a sense of excitement and adventure.

✎ Activity 2.1

Make a recording of your voice during a lesson. Then, with your induction tutor, play back the tape. Try to pick out the good and bad points, e.g.

- are your words clear?
- have you put expression into what you say?
- did you speak too fast?
- is there variation in your tone?

Teacher talk and language

Teachers use talk as their most common teaching method. What are its advantages and disadvantages?

Advantages
- It is a convenient model for delivering an explanation.
- It can be adapted to the correct 'level' for the needs of the class.
- It can be inspiring.
- Little preparation or resourcing is required for the experienced teacher.
- It is a rapid method of presenting material.
- It is a more personal method of communicating than written methods.

Disadvantages
- There is no feedback on whether understanding has taken place.
- The teacher must go at the same pace with the whole class.
- Inexperienced teachers tend to deliver material more quickly.
- It can be boring and there is no active pupil involvement.
- Pupils' concentration span is shorter than for other learning methods.
- It assumes consenting pupils.
- Pupils are not given the opportunity to use the ideas being taught.

(Petty 1998, p. 126)

Teacher talk must be understandable, otherwise there is little point in using it. Waterhouse (1990) urges the use of three basic principles: be simple, be short and be human. In putting these into practice, he claims it is better to choose:

- the concrete noun rather than the abstract;
- the active voice rather than the passive;
- the short sentence rather than the long;
- the simple sentence rather than the compound;
- the direct statement rather than the circumlocution;
- people as the subject wherever possible.

That is not to imply that you should avoid, say, introducing pupils to specialist terminology. On the contrary, it is your responsibility to initiate them in the language of your subject. From the Bullock Report (DES 1975) to the current literacy hour, teachers have been urged to see language as the responsibility of everyone, and not just 'English' staff. However, the use of specialist vocabulary should be developed carefully, with recourse to comparisons, examples, repetition and explanation to ensure children understand ideas and learn them better.

Exposition and explanation

Being able to inform, describe and explain something with clarity is another key communication skill – and it is not your subject knowledge alone that will make you a good explainer. Quite naturally, pupils expect teachers to explain things clearly at their level of understanding. These are some of the necessary ingredients:

Basic skills of explanation
- *Clarity and fluency* – through defining new terms clearly and appropriate use of explicit language.
- *Emphasis and interest* – making good use of voice, gestures, materials and paraphrasing.
- *Using examples* – appropriate in type and quality.
- *Organisation* – presence of a logical sequence and use of link words and phrases.
- *Feedback* – offering a chance for pupils to ask questions and assessing learning outcomes.

(Brown and Armstrong 1984)

The following are some techniques that you could use in attempting to explain concepts or ideas that pupils find difficult or technical, based on the need to make them *easy to remember* and *easy to understand*.

Make explanations easier to remember by:

- simplifying them to include only vital information, leaving the oddities till later;
- focusing on the core of the teaching point one is trying to make, as a key phrase, list or chain of reasoning;
- using everyday language so that the idea is stated in simple terms;
- structuring explanations into easily assimilated portions, with headings, sub-headings and bullet points;
- breaking topics into sensible sections based on the six 'questioning words' – what, why, when, how, where and who.

Make explanations easier to understand by:

- building on pupils' prior knowledge and learning;
- using questioning to encourage pupils to be curious and to interrogate material;

- making visual representations which show 'the whole' at once, e.g. mind maps or flow diagrams;
- begin with concrete examples, so that abstract ideas are introduced through specific points from pupils' own experiences;
- giving summaries that provide an overview of the main ideas and structure.

Questioning

The reasons for questioning being such a familiar and potent feature of classroom life are identified by Brown and Edmondson (1994) as follows:

- to encourage thought, understanding of ideas, phenomena, procedures and values;
- to check understanding, knowledge and skills;
- to gain attention to task – to enable the teacher to move towards teaching points, as a warm-up activity for pupils;
- to review, revise, recall or reinforce a recently learned point – to remind pupils of earlier procedures;
- to teach the whole class through pupil answers;
- to give everyone a chance to answer;
- to draw in shy pupils;
- to probe pupils' knowledge after critical answers;
- to allow expression of feelings, views and empathy.

When considering types of question, you should refer to the six levels of thought process identified in Bloom's Taxonomy (1956), namely: knowledge, comprehension, application, analysis, synthesis and evaluation. This will ensure you identify the thinking level at which pupils are working and give them progressively more challenging questions. And once higher-order mental skills are developed, they are *generally* applicable by pupils.

You should also distinguish between 'open' and 'closed' questions. *Closed questions* involve only one short satisfactory answer and usually concern facts or information that pupils should know, e.g. 'In which year was the first Public Health Act passed?' or 'Who was the first doctor to use anti-smallpox vaccinations?' They can be answered without widening the teacher–pupil dialogue, although they are useful as a 'starter' for more complex open questions or for testing pupils' recall at the end of a lesson.

By contrast, *open questions* are more challenging because they require pupils to explore their own ideas and offer scope for carrying on the line of questioning, e.g. 'To what extent did the Second World War stimulate advances in surgery?' or 'Why is Hippocrates regarded as the father of modern medicine?' In answering these questions, the pupil must think about and apply information – so be prepared to wait for an answer. To structure the dialogue, it is worth using the 'funnelling' technique. This means starting with an open question and then narrowing down the line of questioning in a logical sequence to some definite end that you have in mind.

Questions to avoid are ones that provoke confused replies or blank stares. 'Double', 'kitchen sink', 'fuzzy' and 'jargon' questions are but a few, and their names speak for themselves. Also an interrogatory style will result in a lower response rate, as does cutting your pupil respondent off in mid-sentence. Probing for further details requires skill to ensure it does not become prompting: there is a fine dividing line between clarifying and feeding responses. The final point is to encourage respect for everyone's contributions by never condoning pupils who try to put down others who answer.

It is equally important to consider carefully *how to respond to answers*. For example:

- always praise correct responses, e.g. 'that's right' or 'well done';
- welcome partially correct answers and probe for additional points, e.g. 'good, but

what about...?' or 'you're on the right lines, but could anybody say a little bit more about that?';

- give assistance if it is needed during an answer, e.g. a nod or a word of help or some re-phrasing;
- try to treat seriously incorrect or misdirected answers, e.g. 'I know what you're getting at, but...' or 'that's interesting, but would it work in this case?';
- be open to unexpected or imaginative ideas, e.g. 'great idea: I hadn't thought of that'.

✎ Activity 2.2

Ask your induction tutor to arrange for you to observe a lesson involving a question-and-answer session. Here are some points to note:

- What ground rules are employed (e.g. hands up, only a named person speaking at any one time)?
- Are these routines followed?
- What proportion of hands goes up each time?
- What are the proportions of girls and boys who answer, either voluntarily or when the teacher chooses respondents?
- How does the teacher respond to correct, incorrect and tangential answers?
- How does the pupil respond after giving a correct, incorrect or tangential answer?

After the lesson, you should talk to:

- the teacher
- a pupil who was actively involved
- a pupil who was not much involved

to see what they thought about the questioning and answering.

Discussion

Discussion work often leads on from questioning without a clear demarcation, in that it starts with children who think of their own questions or when one pupil takes up a point that another has made. It is of particular value where:

- pupils' opinions and experiences need to be shared, or known by the teacher;
- topics involve values, attitudes, feelings and awareness;
- it is necessary to give pupils practice in forming and evaluating opinions.

It is possible you might be hesitant about using discussions in case pupils express 'wrong' or 'misguided' views. However, these can be influenced only if they are brought out into the open, giving pupils the chance to examine and reflect on their opinions. Moving beyond a formally taught lesson will show them that you are interested in their views and value their experiences. Also, well-managed discussion provides opportunities for pupils to:

- use higher-level thinking skills, e.g. evaluation and synthesis;
- develop affective qualities, e.g. empathy for other people's viewpoints.

To develop an effective classroom discussion requires *structuring*. Starting off with clear objectives in mind, you should have available some factual material to stimulate debate and a list of key 'open' questions as a framework in which pupils can develop their opinions. Initial questions that are either provocative, or require a response from each pupil, will help get the discussion going. The latter approach is valuable in larger groups, where more assertive pupils (often boys) dominate contributions. Praising children's opinions will encourage responses, as will use of non-verbal body language, e.g. nods, eye contact, smiles, or gestures.

It is important to be in firm control, so establish *ground rules*, e.g. no interrupting or shooting down other pupils' viewpoints. The *seating arrangements* in the classroom are important (e.g. a circle of chairs or seminar layout), so pupils can see and hear each other. Some discussions benefit from being open-ended, although there is the danger they could end up as a shapeless ventilation of views. In this situation, the teacher's *summing-up* is important in reiterating the main points and identifying conclusions, so that pupils are clear about what they have gained from the activity.

Listening

Listening effectively is an important part of a new teacher's communication skills. Good listening means hearing, registering and understanding a pupil's words, and then planning what to say in reply. If done properly, it conveys your respect for what the child has said.

There are several ways in which you can develop effective listening:

- *focusing* – help a pupil keep to the point by latching onto one area of his/her initial response;
- *verbal prompts* – uttering small sounds or expressions of assent encourage a pupil to continue talking or expand on a thought;
- *repeating a key word or point* – doing this in the right tone of voice proves you are listening to the child and taking him/her seriously;
- *silences* – taking a pause (indicated by head nods, eye contact or facial expressions) can give a pupil space to think and then continue talking;
- *paraphrasing* – putting what the pupil has said into your own words shows that you have thought about what you've been told.

There are a number of barriers to good listening. They include:

- failing to listen attentively because you are thinking ahead;
- switching off attention and exhibiting a glassy-eyed look;
- developing a hostility to what you are being told;
- getting distracted by other pupils or extraneous incidents.

Non-verbal communication

Another way of working effectively with pupils involves the use and understanding of non-verbal communication and body language. A new teacher needs to become skilled in quickly picking up the moods of individuals and groups, acknowledging that awareness, and showing pupils he/she can make a timely response. Inappropriate or unreceptive reactions will detract from your control and, consequently, have a negative effect on behaviour.

Appearance

Impressions count for a lot, so the way you look or how you stand in front of a class can have a marked effect on their learning and behaviour. A tidy appearance and appropriate clothing conveys a message to pupils about the authority and competence of your status and role. It also helps to contribute to the attempt staff make, as a whole, to emphasise agreed conventions and expectations. The importance of self-presentation extends to the care you take with board work, resources, marking and other facets of teacher–pupil interaction.

Eagerness and interest

Your ability to convey interest and enthusiasm for studying your subject is vital. Several forms of body language are important here:

- *facial expressions, especially smiles* – these are a sensitive guide to your feelings, in terms of conveying excitement and pleasure about the tasks you expect pupils to undertake;
- *eyes and eyebrows* – these send out a range of messages, implying liking, surprise, alertness, interest – or boredom;
- *gestures* – holding an unseen object in your hands can accompany the presentation of an idea or the wave of one hand can encourage a suggestion;
- *posture* – the way you sit or stand indicates feelings, such as leaning forward in an eager, interested way or sitting defensively with folded arms or crossed legs or drooping in a tired, 'couldn't-care-less' manner;
- *proximity* – how close you position yourself to a pupil can cause discomfort or intimidation.

Confidence and caring

There are several ways that you can convey to pupils a sense of being confident, assured, purposeful and yet relaxed. Kyriacou (1991) stresses that the starting point is sound lesson preparation and tight classroom organisation. This will develop through training and experience. However, speed is of the essence, since children expect teachers to demonstrate confidence and authority from the start. If they sense you are unsure or apprehensive, it is in their nature to test your control for any weaknesses!

Whatever your inner anxieties, Capel *et al.* (1995) argue that you can seek to present yourself with confidence in two main ways:

- *by verbal means*, e.g. clear instructions, purposeful explanations, a firm and measured voice, fluid and well-articulated delivery;
- *by non-verbal means*, e.g. facial expression, regular eye contact with pupils, scanning the classroom, standing centre-stage at the front.

The final point to make is that successful teaching and learning depends on the type of *relationship* a teacher is able to develop with pupils. Research cited by Hill (1996) points to 'teacher warmth' as an important variable in influencing pupil progress. In other words, children prefer teachers who are firm, but also understanding and friendly. You need to show that you care about their progress by planning and conducting effective lessons, and by conveying a sense of respect for each pupil as an individual in their needs and requirements. Therein lies the basis of a genuinely positive classroom climate in which you may develop your professional skills.

> ✎ **Activity 2.3**
> Make a video recording of an accomplished TV presenter, e.g. Jeremy Paxman on *Newsnight.*
>
> As you play it back, make a note of all the different forms of non-verbal communication and body language that are used, as well as actual words. What use is made of pitch, intonation, word or phrase emphasis, pauses during the flow of speech, frowns, smiles, gazing, gesticulations, etc?

Eyes front and think 'boots': will your body language help or hinder your efforts to control a lively classroom?

- *Assume the superior position* – Command the heights of the room. Make sure you are standing up and they are sitting down.
- *Face front* – Teachers tend to write on boards three-quarters turned away from their classes at most. If this is not possible, reframe the lessons to ensure that for the first few weeks at least, you do face front.
- *Stillness* – Pupils sense agitation. Before each class, take time to compose yourself. Remind yourself that you are safe and calm inside.
- *Voice projection* – Relax that throat, lower that vocal range and project. The basic rule is to control the breathing, bring the voice up from your boots and aim it at the back wall.
- *Don't get angry* – Try to see why they are being difficult, refrain from feeding it, and remove the satisfaction by not responding. Don't be threatening: that ups the stakes dramatically.
- *And finally* – Know when to listen. You must set the agenda, but . . . you have to give space for learning and response.

(Neumark 1998, p. 40)

References

Bloom, B. (1956) *Taxonomy of Educational Objectives*. London: Longman.

Brown, G. and Armstrong, S. (1984) 'Explaining and Explanations', in Wragg, E. (ed.) *Classroom Teaching Skills*. London: Croom Helm.

Brown, G. and Edmondson, R. (1984) 'Asking Questions', in Wragg, E. (ed.) *Classroom Teaching Skills*. London: Croom Helm.

Capel, S., Leask, M. and Turner, T. (1995) *Learning To Teach in the Secondary School*. London: Routledge.

DES (1975) *A Language for Life* (The Bullock Report). London: HMSO.

Hill, P. (1996) 'Leadership for Effective Teaching'. Paper presented at the International Principals' Institute, University of Southern California School of Education, Los Angeles (27 July 1996).

Kyriacou, C. (1991) *Essential Teaching Skills*. Hemel Hempstead: Simon & Schuster.

Neumark, V. (1998) 'Eyes front and think boots', *Times Educational Supplement*, 9 January 1998, 40.

Petty, G. (1998) *Teaching Today*. Cheltenham: Stanley Thornes.

Waterhouse, P. (1990) *Classroom Management*. Stafford: Network Educational Press.

Wragg, E. (1984) *Classroom Teaching Skills*. London: Croom Helm.

Chapter 3
Managing behaviour and discipline

Kevan Bleach and Heather McLachlan

Schools must be well-ordered communities if they are to educate children effectively. One of the key ingredients of successful teaching and learning is an atmosphere of care, security and respect, within defined boundaries of behaviour. In this respect, rules have an administrative justification – being time and context specific, as well as moral necessities. Where *mis*behaviour occurs, pupils cannot learn effectively.

Good behaviour and discipline encompass many aspects of schooling – the curriculum, classroom management, attendance, links with parents, pupil–teacher relationships, high expectations by teachers, etc. They are particularly linked to the skills involved in effective teaching in general. In other words, if classroom activities are well planned, if lessons excite and hold pupils' attention and involvement, and if work is challenging and offers tangible and differentiated opportunities for success, good order will be much easier to secure.

Behaviour and discipline, understandably, comprise a strong area of concern for newly qualified teachers, although even the most skilful and experienced teachers encounter problems from time to time. This chapter seeks to help you develop an awareness of causes of misbehaviour and identify ways of improving your ability to deal with behavioural problems in the classroom. It does so under the following headings:

1. The complexities of behaviour and discipline.
2. Insights offered by the Elton Report.
3. Practical strategies for managing misbehaviour.
4. Positive behaviour management schemes.

The complexities of behaviour and discipline

The Elton Report (1989) is the major government report on this topic. One of its main findings was that 'bad behaviour in schools is a complex problem, which does not lend itself to simple solutions'. Partly, this is because there are many *types of misbehaviour*. They range on a continuum from minor irritations (e.g. chatting out of turn, being boisterous, failing to pay attention, lack of concentration, wandering about, interfering with other children, lateness) to more serious forms of disruption (e.g. verbal abuse, insubordination when given clear instructions, vandalism, bullying, racial abuse). Also, teachers' *perceptions of misbehaviour* tend to differ. There is likely to be disagreement about what constitutes minor disruption and how it should be dealt with, which often hinges on differences of personality and style (e.g. insisting on silent working or tolerating 'working noise'). Similarly, pupils vary in their attitudes and expectations.

Some forms of misbehaviour have their origins outside school in the home or peer groups. Within school, factors to do with the curriculum, timetable or rooming may have an influence. Nevertheless, it is important to understand that individual teachers can minimise most minor problems by establishing a positive learning environment with clear expectations of classroom behaviour, which are then rewarded when met or punished when transgressed. The goal is to get children *wanting* to achieve high standards of behaviour to facilitate their learning. This will enable you to develop good relationships with pupils and to practise skilful teaching. However, the ethos of your department and school also has an important role to play in reinforcing a positive learning environment and high expectations of behaviour.

✎ Activity 3.1
Think about different types of pupil misbehaviour that have occurred in classes you have taught or observed. Sort them into categories (e.g. noise, misuse of equipment, movement, verbal, physical).
Then discuss with your induction tutor how each type of misbehaviour should be responded to. What could you have done to pre-empt such misconduct?

The main *causes of misbehaviour* have been summarised by Kyriacou (1991) and Capel *et al.* (1995) as follows:

- *boredom* – failing to offer classroom activities that are interesting, appropriately timed, challenging and relevant;
- *poor teacher organisation* – visual aids do not work or there are too many interruptions to the flow of the lesson;
- *confusion about teacher expectations* – the teacher fails to be clear and explicit about the kind of conduct that is expected;
- *inability to do the work set* – because it is too difficult, expressed in inappropriate language or it is unclear what pupils need to do;
- *prolonged mental effort* – which is difficult to sustain over a long period;
- *seeking attention* – sometimes bad behaviour is the only way to secure a teacher's attention;
- *social or peer interaction* – conversations or behaviour can spill over into the classroom from the corridor, playground or outside school;
- *low academic self-esteem* – alienation occurs where pupils lack confidence in themselves because they have experienced failure before;
- *emotional difficulties* – bullying in school or neglect at home may make it difficult to adjust to the demands of the classroom;
- *unacceptable social attitudes* – some pupils' family or social values are different from those of their school.

✎ Activity 3.2
Here are some issues to discuss with your induction tutor about the daily practical aspects of behaviour and discipline:

- Are there specific locations in the school (e.g. toilets, exits, bike sheds, dining room, corridors) where misbehaviour is more likely to occur?
- Are there times of the day when classes are more difficult to control?
- Are there any clusters of pupils who behave poorly in the school?
- What behaviour do you find most distressing in your lesson?
- What should be done if you find a pupil trading abuse with another?
- What are the ways in which you give praise and rewards?
- What hierarchy of reprimands or sanctions do you use?

- What expectations does the school have if pupils are taken on visits?
- What should be done if a child's behaviour in class goes out of control?
- In what situations have you called on the support of someone else?
- What should you do if a parent complains about your treatment of his/her child?
- What should you do if some pupils mess around when sent off to work on their own?
- Do boys and girls differ in their behaviour?
- What do you do if any pupils are being bullied by others?
- Which teachers in the school do you admire for their skill in managing pupil behaviour, and why?

Insights offered by the Elton Report

Concern about behaviour in schools in the 1980s motivated the government of that time to ask Lord Elton to investigate and report on the issue. The Elton Report of 1989, *Discipline in Schools*, drives much of our thinking in schools today, in that it provides valuable insights into behaviour and recommendations about improving discipline.

The Report contains 292 pages and 132 recommendations for teachers, schools, LEAs, parents, pupils and governors. It argues that discipline is a complex issue which needs complex strategies – particularly if the kind of environment in which all pupils can flourish, and all can come to school without fear, is to be created. That is why a team approach, framed within a whole-school policy, is essential. The management of behaviour is the responsibility of *everyone* in the school.

Here are some extracts from the Report of particular relevance to NQTs:

Classroom Management

- In order to learn well, children need a calm and purposeful atmosphere... Teachers must be able to keep order...They should not face this task alone. They need and deserve support.
- Teachers see talking out of turn and other forms of persistent, low-level disruptive behaviour as the most frequent and wearing kinds.
- Teachers with good group management skills are able to establish positive relationships with their classes based on mutual respect. They can create a climate in which pupils lose rather than gain popularity with their classmates by causing trouble. They can also spot a disruptive incident in the making, choose an appropriate tactic to deal with it and nip it in the bud... They model the good behaviour they expect from pupils.
- There are teachers who lack confidence in their own ability to deal with disruption and who see classes as potentially hostile. They create a negative classroom atmosphere by frequent criticism and rare praise. They make use of loud reprimands and threats. They are sometimes sarcastic. They tend to react aggressively to minor incidents.
- A common belief is that group management skills are simply a natural gift. You either have it or you don't...Its most damaging feature is that teachers who have difficulty in controlling classes tend to put this down to personal inadequacy rather than to lack of particular skills that can be acquired through training or advice from colleagues...
- Although there are some differences in detail, there is a high degree of agreement in the literature about the main features of good practice. There is always general agreement that well organised and delivered lessons help secure good standards of behaviour. Some of the clearest messages are that teachers should:

---

1. *Know their pupils as individuals. This means knowing their names, their personalities and interests and who their friends are.*

2. *Plan and organise both the classroom and the lesson to keep pupils interested and minimise the opportunities for disruption. This requires attention to such basics as furniture layout, grouping of pupils, matching work to pupils' abilities, pacing the lesson well, being enthusiastic and using humour to create a positive classroom atmosphere.*

3. *Be flexible in order to take advantage of unexpected events, rather than being thrown off balance by them.*

4. *Continually observe or 'scan' the classroom.*

5. *Be aware of and control their behaviour, including tone of voice.*

6. *Model the standards of courtesy they expect from pupils.*

7. *Emphasise the positive, including praise for good behaviour and work.*

8. *Make the rules for classroom behaviour clear to pupils from the first lesson and explain why they are necessary.*

9. *Make sparing and consistent use of reprimands. This means being firm rather than aggressive, criticising the behaviour not the person, using private rather than public reprimands wherever possible, being fair and consistent, and avoiding sarcasm and idle threats.*

10. *Make sparing and consistent use of punishments. This includes avoiding whole-group punishments which pupils see as unfair. It also means avoiding punishments which humiliate pupils by, for example, making them look ridiculous.*

11. *Analyse their own class management performance and learn from it. This is the most important message of all.*

(DES 1989)

✎ **Activity 3.3**

Discuss with your induction tutor the implications for your classroom management of the above extracts from Elton.
Reflect on a recent incident of pupil misbehaviour:

- what was the cause of the misbehaviour?
- how might it have been anticipated and prevented?
- how would you deal with it in the light of Elton's recommendations?

Practical strategies for managing misbehaviour

So what are the ways in which new teachers can deal with pupil behaviour? In minimising opportunities for misconduct, the extent to which your organisational and teaching strategies are well rehearsed will have a positive impact. If, for instance, you have clearly established your expectations regarding classroom routines and carefully planned the use of your time for teaching the whole class and moving between individuals and groups to question, explain and assess, then your prospects for successfully managing behaviour look good.

Kyriacou (1991) suggests several useful ways of *preventing misbehaviour*:

Scan the classroom	See if any pupils are having difficulties and support them in resuming working quickly. Individual contact is more effective than calling across the room.
Circulate	Go round the room asking pupils about their progress. This uncovers problems which otherwise would not be obvious.
Make eye contact	Do this with individuals when talking to the class. Prolonged eye contact shows a pupil he/she should become re-involved, without having to interrupt the lesson.
Target your questions	Directing questions around the class keeps pupils involved. Targeting questions at individuals keeps them attentive.
Use proximity	Moving towards pupils who are talking indicates awareness of their conduct. Standing by pupils keeps them on task.
Give academic help	This encourages pupils to make progress with the task set and is one of the best ways of pre-empting misbehaviour.
Change activities or pace	Sometimes lessons proceed too slowly or too fast, so altering the activity or pace can be crucial for maintaining pupils' involvement.
Notice mis-behaviour	Use eye contact, facial expressions and pauses to signal disapproval, so there's only a momentary interruption of the lesson. Ignoring trivial incidents allows more serious misbehaviour to occur.
Notice disrespect	Discourtesy to you, as teacher, must be picked up or it will undermine the standard of behaviour expected from pupils.
Move pupils	If necessary, separate pupils whose behaviour is not acceptable, while stressing it is done in their interests.

(Abridged from Kyriacou 1991, pp. 89-90)

If misbehaviour still occurs, you will need to consider what steps to take in terms of rebuking the offending pupil(s). Again, Kyriacou (1991) offers sound advice on the effective *use of reprimands*:

Correct targeting	It is important to identify correctly the pupil who is responsible for misbehaviour.
Firmness	Use a clear and firm tone. Avoid pleading or softening the reprimand once it is issued.
Express concern	Reprimands should convey your concern with the pupil's interests or those of other pupils affected by misconduct.
Avoid anger	Don't lose your cool, whatever the provocation. Speak assertively, not aggressively, and do not rise to any bait.
Emphasise what is required	Stress what pupils *should* be doing rather than complain about bad behaviour, e.g. 'You may talk *quietly* with your neighbour' is better than 'There's too much noise in here'.
Psychological impact	Retain impact during a reprimand by means of non-verbal cues like eye contact or a slight pause.
Avoid confrontations	Where pupils are agitated, counselling can be more effective. Where there is likely to be an emotional reaction, postpone the reprimand till the end of the lesson.

Criticise behaviour, not the pupil	Disapprove the conduct, rather than the individual. It provides an opening for the pupil to avoid future misbehaviour.
Use private, not public reprimands	If you talk to an offender away from the class, it increases personal contact and lessens the likelihood of arousing the hostility born of public embarrassment.
Pre-emptive	Reprimands aimed at pre-empting misconduct are more effective than those following repeated bad behaviour.
State rules and rationale	State which rule is being broken, followed by an explanation of why it is needed, e.g. 'John, I need you to stop talking so I can explain to the class what I want them to do'.
Avoid making hostile remarks	Deprecating remarks are taken personally by pupils. Making them public victims of your wit undermines the respect needed for a positive climate.
Avoid unfair comparisons	Stereotyping or comparisons with other pupils, particularly a brother or sister, are unfair, e.g. 'I suppose it's too much to expect a set five pupil to be able to do this problem'.
Be consistent	A pupil will resent being treated in a way that is perceived to be different from another child. The severity of a reprimand should not be unfair.
Do not make empty threats	Say what you mean and mean what you say! If sanctions are threatened, they must be carried out or one's credibility will be lost, e.g. 'If you make another insolent remark, I shall be phoning home'.
Avoid reprimanding the whole class	This should be done only if misbehaviour is so widespread that individual reprimands are inappropriate. To avoid casting criticism on the blameless, express concern about 'too many pupils' misbehaving.
Make an example	Reprimanding an individual, and adding that you will not tolerate other pupils acting in this way, can be useful in the first few lessons with a new class to highlight expectations.

(Abridged from Kyriacou 1991, pp. 92–6)

The ability to manage pupils on an individual, group or class basis is one of the main causes of anxiety that newly qualified teachers suffer from at the beginning of their induction year. However, you should take reassurance from the fact that your first response to minor misbehaviour will probably be sufficient to restore order so long as it is typified by calm assurance and a positive manner. Research shows that the misbehaviour most commonly faced by primary and secondary teachers is relatively trivial. For example, the Elton Report indicated that 'talking out of turn' was the most common problem. All the suggestions given above offer you a variety of fairly light, non-intrusive interventions. The ones you choose to employ will be contingent on particular circumstances. The success of each one, realistically, will vary from teacher to teacher and situation to situation.

Where reprimands do *not* work, it is necessary to use *punishments* to counter misbehaviour. To be effective, punishments should embody the following points:

- *focus on the misdeed* – avoid personalised punishments so that the pupil is forced to consider the consequences of his/her action;
- *follow promptly after the offence* – punishment will be more effective in modifying behaviour if it follows immediately, although deferral can be effective if it causes an unpleasant anticipation of what is likely to happen;

- *be consistent* – pupils have a strong sense of grievance about variations in treatment either between individuals or between occasions;
- *fit the crime* – the scale of punishment used should demonstrate the seriousness of the offence and the strength of the school's disapproval;
- *be followed by reconciliation* – once a punishment is over, attempt to rebuild a positive relationship with the pupil.

✎ Activity 3.4

Think about the following questions on ways of punishing pupils:

- What punishments do you use at present? Rate each one on a 1–5 scale, with low numbers indicating greater effectiveness.
- What punishments do you find yourself using more frequently than others?
- Have you ever explored pupils' opinions about punishments? If so, did it throw up any surprises?
- Are there any punishments you deliberately do not use? Why?

Now discuss your views with your induction tutor.

Positive behaviour management schemes

Increasingly, schools realise that discipline cannot safely be left to the vagaries of individual teachers. A positive attitude towards behaviour and work is best maintained by a team effort, which in turn is a product of a whole-school policy and training.

Many schools have drawn on research and use training packages from LEAs and other sources to create their policies. Individual schools have their own emphases, but the main ingredients are remarkably similar. Common to all current approaches, for example, is an emphasis on *praising and rewarding good behaviour*. Expressing appreciation for acceptable conduct, rather than merely taking it for granted, increases the chance of it reoccurring. Schools may have a range of available rewards – e.g. behaviour/achievement stamps/stickers, letters home, merit awards, certificates, prizes, visits – although thought has to be given to what is credible with individual pupils if they are to be effective.

Research shows that if teachers give more positive attention to pupils' behaviour, it actually improves. Michael Barber (OFSTED/SCAA/TTA 1996) urges us to try to ensure a three-to-one ratio of praise to criticism, with encouragement focusing on specific examples of good performance to raise expectations and develop self-esteem.

Always accentuate the positive

- 'Rules, praise and ignoring' is a very robust strategy in which teachers first negotiate with their pupils a few positively phrased rules for the classroom. The teacher thus puts emphasis on those who keep the rules rather than those who do not...
- Systematic manipulation of classroom seating arrangements can be very effective in bringing about a higher level of on-task behaviour and, at the same time, improving work output.
- Quiet, private reprimands have been shown to be more effective than loud, public reprimands with older pupils. 'A noisy teacher makes a noisy class' is an old dictum that is still true.

(Merrett 1994, p. 7)

Assertive discipline

This is a system that has influenced many UK schools and is endorsed by the DfEE. It was developed by the American teacher and educationalist, Lee Canter (1976). As well as stressing the need for frequent reinforcement of good behaviour, it puts great emphasis on a *hierarchy of sanctions* that must be consistently adhered to. Many schools negotiate these penalties with pupils, arguing that this is more democratic and gives pupils a sense of ownership.

CASE STUDY
Classroom Behaviour Plan

'The TEACHER has the right to TEACH and STUDENTS have the right to LEARN' (Lee Canter)

RULES
- Students will follow teachers' instructions the first time they are given.
- When a teacher or student is speaking, the students will listen in silence.
- Students will indicate when they want to speak, and will wait to be asked before speaking.
- Students will not eat or drink in class.

REWARDS
- Praise.
- Praise and a behaviour stamp.
- Letter or telephone call home.
- Referral to the Head of Department, Form Tutor or Year Tutor.
- Special awards.

CONSEQUENCES
- A warning – logged by class teacher.
- Student to be last to leave the classroom and kept to perform a two-minute task, e.g. to put up the chairs or tidy the classroom.
- Ten minute detention immediately after the lesson.
- After-school or lunchtime detention of 35 minutes organised by the Department concerned.
- A letter to parents from the Head of Department, the student's Form Tutor or Head of Year.
- The severe clause.*

* This clause is invoked in severe cases of misbehaviour and disruption in the classroom and involves the use of a First Call teacher who will make contact with the subject teacher and arrange to extract the offender(s) from the room.

(St Thomas More Catholic Comprehensive School, Walsall)

What Assertive Discipline aims to do is draw together the basic requirements for classroom management into a systematic discipline plan that *all* teachers can use. In addition, it deals with the emotional motivation of teachers to implement such a plan by *asserting their right to teach* – hence the name of the programme. It stresses that assertive discipline must be integrated into the teacher's routine teaching, becoming fundamental to the classroom atmosphere and not something bolted on just for disruptive pupils. In the words of Lee Canter, 'Today you must come to class prepared not only to teach... but to motivate students to behave appropriately as well.'

The Case Study shows how one school has introduced a *Classroom Behaviour Plan* as part of its implementation of Assertive Discipline. This plan reflects the whole-school behaviour plan and copies are displayed in every room. Staff teach the plan to pupils from the first lesson. Since consistency is a crucial factor in its implementation, guidelines have been drawn up for the use of rewards and consequences.

References

Canter, L. and Canter, A. (1976) *Assertive Discipline.* Seal Beach: Canter Associates.

Capel, S., Leask, M. and Turner, T. (1995) *Learning to Teach in the Secondary School.* London: Routledge.

DES (1989) *Discipline in Schools. Report of the Committee of Enquiry Chaired by Lord Elton.* London: HMSO/DES.

Kyriacou, C. (1991) *Essential Teaching Skills.* Hemel Hempstead: Simon & Schuster.

Merrett, F. (1994) 'Always accentuate the positive', *Times Educational Supplement,* 14 January 1994, 7.

OFSTED/SCAA/TTA (1996) *Teachers Make a Difference: Post-Conference Report.* London: OFSTED/SCAA/TTA.

Chapter 4

Systematic approaches to classroom management

Christopher Arnold

The use of systematic, school-wide approaches to behaviour management is increasing. The DfEE have mentioned 'Assertive Discipline' in their reports of good practice. Although this is the name of a commercial package originating from the United States, a number of schemes have emerged, some of which use the same terminology and principles. Lee Canter noted in a recent visit to the UK that 'Assertive Discipline' has become a generic term, much as the word 'Hoover' describes vacuum cleaners made by other manufacturers.

These ideas are finding their way onto initial teacher training courses, albeit slowly. Ten years ago, less than ten per cent of newly qualified teachers in secondary schools reported that they had received training in systematic approaches to behaviour management. By 1999, that figure had increased to fifty per cent.

This chapter aims to summarise the principles of positive behaviour management that may assist you as a new teacher. It addresses the following areas:

1. What are my class rules?
2. How do I reinforce the rules?
3. How do I give directions to the class?
4. How do I correct children who choose not to follow the rules?
5. Behaving assertively in your interactions with children
6. Checklist for problem-solving.

What are my class rules?

Rules form the first part of your discipline plan. The first step in getting to grips with undesirable behaviour is to choose rules that tell pupils what they should be doing, i.e. the *desirable behaviour*. Doing this is greatly simplified once it is realised that all problems faced in the classroom can fall into one of the following categories:

- relations with adults and peers
- academic work
- classroom routines
- relations to self
- safety.

Similarly, the rules you generate will fall into these five categories.

Three important points to remember about rules are:

- if you don't need it, don't bother to use it;
- only use positive rules that tell pupils what they can do, rather than what they can't do (otherwise you risk putting ideas into their heads!);
- use a maximum of five rules.

Using positive rules has a number of advantages:

- they make your expectations clear to the class;
- they act as reminders to both you and the class regarding what standards are expected;
- they make it easier for you to know what to say to the class when you are using praise.

Rules may be more effective if they are generated through negotiation and discussion with your class. In this way, the pupils have ownership of them too. Think about:

- how you would plan a lesson to discuss and formulate rules;
- how to display rules in the classroom: this might vary according to the age of your pupils.

It is vital to remember that concern with specific behaviours can result in too many rules. Four or five per classroom is sufficient. The following is one way of categorising behaviours into rules. There are other possibilities.

Five categories of rules	
1. Relations with adults and peers	a. be polite and friendly b. be friendly and helpful c. help your friends
2. Academic work	a. work hard and quietly b. do your best c. try
3. Classroom routines	a. put your hand up b. settle down quickly and quietly c. stay in your seat
4. Relations to self	a. respect yourself b. be smart c. accept your own and others' mistakes d. keep trying e. you can do it
5. Safety	a. take care b. be safe c. take care of your friends' safety

How do I reinforce the rules?

Rewards form the second part of the classroom discipline plan. The principle of using rewards, linked with children's good behaviour, underpins positive behaviour management. Consider what rewards are available to you that you can link to good behaviour and jot them down on a piece of paper.

A particular type of reward is, quite simply, praise. It is possible to use positive comments to help children behave better. Within most systems, the wording of positive rules can be used to encourage children to follow them by using 'praise with feedback'.

The following sequence can help:

- gain attention (e.g. 'Brian')
- show approval (e.g. 'well done')
- echo the rules or describe the desired actions (e.g. 'you cooperated really well').

Finding opportunities to do this frequently is worth practising. Successful teachers do not take good behaviour for granted. They teach it!

How do I give directions to the class?

There are something like three hundred different routines that pupils have to learn in school. The use of rules to cover these situations would lead to far too many. Clear, positively phrased directions, backed up with positive feedback, are going to help reduce uncertainty for children.

A useful sequence is:

- gain attention
- describe clearly what you want
- describe what the consequence is likely to be for the pupils
- include a motivational challenge
- start using praise that echoes the instruction you have given as soon as you can.

Here are some examples of directions with praise. Each sentence spoken by the teacher is numbered. The numbers correspond to the five steps involved in delivering directions with praise.

Example 1

1. Listen to me, class.
2. I want you to produce some really neat work, using full stops and capital letters.
3. That will tell me that you've gone a long way towards mastering the skills you need for your exam.
4. How many of you think you can do that? Yes, I think you can, as well.
5. That's neat writing Anna, well done. Everyone on this table is remembering to use full stops, as well.

Example 2

1. Now then, class 3 . . .
2. I want you to take care using the tools and remember to use them safely.
3. If you do that, I'll know I can trust you to use the lathe next week.
4. Do you think you can do that? So do I.
5. Well done, this group. You are being very careful with these tools.

How do I correct children who choose not to follow the rules?

Correction measures form the third part of the discipline plan. Most schools will have a policy on correcting children. It is important that any system is compatible with the school policy. However, it is more likely to be successful if it is displayed alongside the 'rules and rewards' in the Classroom Discipline Plan.

A sample scheme is:

- warning – recorded by teacher
- two minutes away from the group
- five minutes away from the group
- detention
- letter to parents.

Example of a Classroom Discipline Plan

Rules
- Follow teacher directions first time
- Keep hands, feet and objects to yourselves
- Be polite and friendly
- Work hard

Rewards
- Praise
- House point
- Commendations
- Good behaviour awards
- Positive letters home
- Raffle tickets

Corrections
- Warning
- 2 minutes away from the group
- 10 minutes away from the group
- Interview with Head of House/Year/Department
- Parents called in

Behaving assertively in your interactions with children

It is possible to identify different response styles: non-assertive, aggressive and assertive. These are not personality types, but simply different ways of responding to children. They are described in Table 4.1.

It is important to remain calm when dealing with children who are posing management difficulties. Make eye contact, approach the pupil and state clearly what you want them to do. If they begin to argue, say 'I understand, and I need you to...'. If a child persists in arguing, offer a choice: conform or choose a correction. The discipline plan will help you remain assertive.

Table 4.1 A comparison of non-assertive, aggressive and assertive behaviour

	Non-assertive	**Aggressive**	**Assertive**
Characteristics of the behaviour.	Does not express wants, ideas and feelings or expresses them in self-depreciating way. Intent: to please.	Expresses wants, ideas, feelings at the expense of others. Intent: to dominate or humiliate.	Expresses wants, ideas and feelings in direct and appropriate ways. Intent: to communicate.
Your feelings when you act this way.	Anxious, disappointed with yourself. Often angry and resentful later.	Self-righteous, superior. Sometimes embarrassed later.	Confident, feel good about yourself at the time and later.
Other people's feelings about themselves when you act this way.	Guilty or superior.	Humiliated, hurt.	Respected, valued.
Other people's feelings about you when you act this way.	Irritation, pity, disgust.	Angry, vengeful.	Usually respect.
Outcome.	Don't get what you want. Anger builds up.	Often get what you want at the expense of others. Others feel justified at 'getting even'.	Often get what you want.
Pay-off.	Avoids unpleasant situation. Avoids conflict, tension, confrontation.	Vents anger, feels superior.	Feels good, respected by others. Improved self-confidence. Relationships are improved.

(Jakubowski and Lange 1978, p. 42)

Introduction

The purpose of the checklist on pages 33–39 is for you to assess a pupil's learning environment and identify particular antecedents affecting the pupil's behaviour. The antecedents cover environmental factors and classroom management factors.

To complete the checklist (after having carried out the preliminary activity on page 32), tick off relevant antecedents and make notes. Not all the statements may apply to the pupil, so just tick the relevant ones. You may complete the checklist by observing the pupil or by discussion with other members of staff or based on your own knowledge of the pupil.

Having completed the checklist, you should be able to identify particular antecedents affecting a pupil's behaviour. Then you can pinpoint which antecedents to try to change in formulating an Individual Behaviour Plan.

Form for preliminary activity

The timetable	Comments
1. Is there a balance of subjects within a day?	
2. Is there a mix of practical and theoretical lessons?	
3. Are room changes kept to a minimum?	
4. When do problems occur? (Specify day of week/lessons as appropriate)	
5. Where do problems occur? (Location)	

Checklist for problem-solving

Factors	Yes; No; N/A	Comments
Section A: Rules *Is there evidence of the following?*		
1. Rules are kept few in number and clearly phrased.		
2. Rules are positively stated.		
3. Rules are regularly referred to and reinforced.		
4. Rules are clearly displayed in the classroom.		
5. Rules are set for: • work skills • relationships with other pupils • classroom routines • relationship to teacher • safety (e.g. equipment).		
6. Have any of the rules been negotiated with the pupils?		
7. Could the rules apply throughout the day?		
8. Are the rules understood by pupils?		
9. Are the rules relevant to the level of maturity of the pupils?		

Factors	Yes; No; N/A	Comments

Section B:
 Directions/Instructions
 Does the teacher do the following?
 	
 10. Gain pupils' attention before giving directions.
 	
 11. Give clear instructions.
 	
 12. Use MINT in giving directions.
 	
   • **M**aterials – pupils know what is needed
   • **I**n/out of seat (controls movement)
   • **N**oise levels – rules about acceptable noise level are specified
   • **T**ime – time for task specified.
 	
 13. Praise pupils who follow the directions.		

Section C: **Language considerations** *Does the teacher...* 14. Have a clear voice? 15. Use language appropriate to pupils' understanding? 16. Use demonstration and repetition to clarify? 17. Give reminders in a respectful way? 18. Allow pupils to use their existing knowledge? 19. Empower pupils to say if they don't understand?		

Factors	Yes; No; N/A	Comments
Section D: Lesson organisation **BEGINNING OF LESSON** *Is there evidence of the following?* 20. Preparation (homework marked, materials ready). 21. Clear routines taught about entry to class. 22. Teacher arrives before pupils and greets them. 23. Clear start to lesson to get on task immediately. 24. Clear statement of objectives for lesson. **DURING THE LESSON** *Does the teacher do any of the following?* 25. Use brief, random questions. 26. Give clear instructions, particularly between different activities. 27. Use a variety of teaching methods and media. 28. Use a mixture of activities. 29. Deal swiftly and effectively with minor misdemeanours.		

Factors	Yes; No; N/A	Comments
Section D: (continued)		
END OF THE LESSON *Does the teacher do any of the* *following?*		
30. Stop a few minutes before the end.		
31. Give homework if appropriate.		
32. Ensure equipment, etc., is tidied up.		
33. Give a summary of what has been covered.		
34. Reinforce pupils on their performance.		
35. Have clear routines for dismissal.		
Section E: **Seating arrangements** *When grouping pupils, are the* *following taken into account?*		
36. Nature of task (groups v. rows).		
37. Composition of group (e.g. gender mix).		
38. Ground rules for group.		
39. Size of group.		
Section F: **Curriculum consideration** *Would any of the following* *have an effect on the pupil* *behaviour?*		
40. Teaching and learning methods.		
41. Relevance of the curriculum.		
42. Cultural messages (hidden curriculum).		

Factors	Yes; No; N/A	Comments
Section G: **Specific techniques to add security/stability** *Is there evidence of any of the following?* 43. Planning for changes in routine. 44. Setting precise targets covering: • exactly what to do • how much work • for how long • what to do when task is complete.		
Section H: **Positive classroom atmosphere** *Is there evidence of any of the following?* 45. Positive expectations. 46. Praise for following rules/directions. 47. Positive relations between pupils and staff.		
Section I: Managing space 48. Are there clear pathways, e.g. to the door, resource area, etc.? 49. Does the teacher consider pupils' own personal space (cultural/gender issues)? 50. Is the teacher visible at all times? 51. Are the needs of pupils with visual or hearing difficulties considered?		

Factors	Yes; No; N/A	Comments

Section J:
Managing equipment and
apparatus
Are the following taken into
account?
 	
52. Equipment is easily
       accessible.
 	
53. Materials are well labelled
       and located.
 	
54. Appropriate storage of
       pupils' belongings.
 	
55. Chalkboard/whiteboard, etc.,
       easily seen.
 	
56. Someone has responsibility
       for maintenance of equipment.		

Section K:
Creating a good work
environment
Do the following encourage a
positive working environment?
 	
57. Quality of decoration
       and displays.
 	
58. Calming effects (pale
       colours/music).
 	
59. Few distractions/confusing
       features.
 	
60. Appropriate noise level
       in class.
 	
61. Quiet external environment.
 	
62. Sufficient ventilation.
 	
63. Appropriate ambient
       temperature.
 	
64. Lighting sufficient.
 	
65. No glare.
 	
66. Furniture suitable.		

Factors	Yes; No; N/A	Comments
Section L: **Support staff** *Is there evidence of the following for support staff?* 67. Clear job specifications. 68. Task matched to their skills and the expectations of them is clearly communicated. 69. Time for joint planning and preparations. 70. Being involved in the Discipline Plan, so their role is clear.		
Other comments		

Reference

Jakubowski, P. and Lange, A. (1978) *The Assertive Option: Your Rights and Responsibilities.* USA: Research Press.

Chapter 5

Differentiation and effective teaching

The implementation, and later revisions, of the National Curriculum have emphasised *what* to teach, rather than *how* to teach. Yet it is vitally important to ensure that what is taught in the classroom effectively meets the learning needs of pupils. In any class – whether setted or mixed ability – children will exhibit a variety of abilities, aptitudes and needs. The challenge for the newly qualified teacher is to find manageable ways of accommodating these differences, so that the individual pupil is able to realise his/her full potential and achieve the highest standards. Hence, the importance of 'differentiation' as a planned process of intervention in each pupil's classroom learning.

This chapter does not claim to have all the answers about the differentiation of curriculum planning and delivery. However, in addressing the headings below, it seeks to stimulate thought and point you in directions that should prove professionally worthwhile:

1. Defining 'differentiation'
2. Why differentiation matters
3. How differentiation can be achieved
4. How classroom management can help differentiation

Defining 'differentiation'

The term 'differentiation' originally referred to techniques used in assessing pupils to discriminate between their different levels of knowledge and understanding. The first generation of GCSE examinations in the late-1980s popularised the word. Differentiation then featured as one of the National Curriculum's key dimensions, along with breadth, balance, relevance, progression and continuity.

If we hack through the undergrowth of definition and explanation, differentiation can be summarised as the *recognition that pupils tend to learn in different ways and at different speeds*. Indeed, each individual learns in a variety of ways. Also, within any class or group you will find there are marked variations in the levels of children's attainment and the learning difficulties they experience.

Differentiation, therefore, is the process through which you seek to respond to this challenge. It will help you ensure pupils progress through the curriculum, at a pace appropriate to each, by selecting suitable teaching methods and resources that match an individual's learning needs within a group situation. It is a strategy that has always been implicitly at the heart of effective teaching and learning.

It is self-evident to say that all pupils are different. Yet it is amazing how frequently teachers behave as if they were the *same* by pitching delivery in the middle. The spread of abilities and aptitudes in any class is actually quite noticeable. What differentiation seeks to do, as Visser (1993) notes, is address this diversity. The method of grouping you employ may lessen or widen diversity in one way or another, but it will not remove it. Some of the differences that characterise pupil diversity are of no consequence to learning and so will not directly affect your teaching. Others will, thereby affecting the outcome expected and achieved, the task set and the input made to the lesson.

Differentiation is...

- the process of identifying, with each learner, the most effective strategies for achieving agreed targets (Weston 1992)
- a strategy which enables teachers to approach the ideal of a person-to-person encounter in a situation in which resources are constrained, the unlearned many and the wise over-stretched by the diversity of demands put upon them (Belfast Education & Libraries Board 1990)
- the identification of and effective provision for a range of abilities in one classroom, so pupils in a particular class need not study the same things at the same pace and in the same way at all times (Simpson 1989)
- the separation and ranking of students according to a multiple set of criteria (Lacey 1970)

(Visser 1993, p. 17)

It is appropriate to echo the OFSTED view that teachers do not always take into consideration the differences between pupils found in their classes. This has an impact on both ends of the ability spectrum. Allowing pupils to work to a norm, rather than responding positively to their differences, leads inevitably to mediocrity! Part of the key to unlocking the door to a differentiated approach, genuinely catering for the differing talents of children, will be for you to recognise the different learning styles pupils utilise when acquiring skills, knowledge and understanding.

So differentiation is about how you teach and provide for pupils' individual needs in lessons and schemes of work. It is *not* about the individualisation of curriculum content, as that would be a superhuman task. Teachers teach mainly in *groups*, so differentiation must be placed in this context, even though individual provision is sometimes necessary. The challenge for you is to find and provide suitable opportunities for offering differentiated learning experiences. To match your teaching to children's various ways of learning, it is crucial to have a clear understanding of the purposes of differentiation and how it can be professionally implemented in the classroom.

✎ Activity 5.1

List ten differences exhibited by children you teach. Here are some examples:

- ability with a specific skill
- hearing or visual impairment
- left handed
- sees little point in school work
- untidy worker
- fails to see he/she is making progress
- says what he/she thinks, simply and directly
- thrives on the challenge of tackling something new and different
- quiet and thoughtful, perhaps lacking in confidence
- tends to talk more than he/she listens

Now think about the effect that each of these differences would have on your teaching. Some differences will matter more than others. They will affect the *outcome* you expect, the *task* you set and your *input* in the lesson.

Identify how you would try to take account of these differences when planning your teaching.

Why differentiation matters

The differences that exist between pupils require differentiated teaching and learning experiences. By developing and implementing differentiated approaches and activities, you can improve the quality of educational provision in your classroom and reduce the likelihood of pupil failure. *Effective teaching, therefore, is the core purpose of differentiation.* In addition, as Stradling and Saunders (1993) note, differentiation is a means of responding to a number of contemporary educational considerations and requirements:

The demands of the National Curriculum – National Curriculum assessment requirements have prompted schools to adapt practice and resources so that all pupils have effective access to programmes of study. Although schools are now offering more vocationally based courses in Key Stage 4 and can 'disapply' some subjects, children should not be denied access to a broad and balanced curriculum. Part of one's teaching task is to enable them to access their entitlement successfully.

SATs and GCSEs – To meet the needs of pupils with different levels of ability, there are tiered SATs and the vast majority of GCSE courses have tiered papers. This makes differentiation by entry and task the norm.

Debates about teaching methods – A receptive climate for differentiation has been created by the debate over whole-class versus group/individualised teaching, mixed-ability versus setted classes, etc. No one method – whether 'traditional' or 'progressive' – is likely to be effective for all pupils all of the time. Differentiation is a response to the need for variety and appropriateness.

Publication of school examination results – Many parents judge schools on pupils' results without setting in context the raw data that appears in league tables. So the extent to which schools raise standards by effectively maximising each individual's potential is crucial to their success. We cannot escape from the competitive environment in which schools now operate.

Concerns about discipline and behaviour – Pupils' behaviour can be affected by the way teachers teach. The Elton Report (DES 1989) identified disruptiveness as partly arising from some pupils finding their self-esteem threatened by failure. An obvious problem arises when children are entered for academic races in which they are not equipped to take part. Races should be winnable! This sentiment was echoed in the OFSTED report on access and achievement in urban education (1993), which observed that teachers need to adjust their teaching strategies to take account of low reading levels. Of course, this is not to say that there are no behaviour problems in differentiated lessons. Rather, poorly differentiated lessons exacerbate the situation.

Special needs provision – The need for teachers to differentiate effectively has been highlighted by the SEN Code of Practice in terms of assessing pupils' needs and making sure those needs are met. Although not protected by statutory requirements, pupils at the opposite end of the ability range also have 'special needs'. The curriculum followed by the most able pupils should provide sufficient challenge and opportunity for development. Responding to the needs of this group is an important necessity for any school.

OFSTED inspections – These have put differentiation right at the top of the agenda, in terms of the emphasis they place on standards of achievement, quality of learning, curriculum provision, quality of teaching, equality of opportunity, SEN provision and resources. Teachers, including NQTs, *must* be aware of what OFSTED teams will be looking for regarding the quality of teaching and learning.

Behaviour and differentiation

We point out the links between the content and methods of delivery of the school's curriculum, and the motivation and behaviour of pupils, particularly those who are not successful academically... [They require] stimulating and suitably differentiated programmes of study.

(DES 1989, p. 13)

How differentiation can be achieved

Grouping strategies, such as banding or setting, are the traditional way of implementing differentiation. However, they do not do sufficient justice to the differing and changing needs of individual pupils across their whole curriculum. So what you should be thinking about is approaching differentiation in terms of maximising the motivation, progress and achievement of each individual pupil, as far as is practicable. In other words, as Stradling and Saunders (1993) observe, it should be addressed as a teaching, rather than merely an organisational, strategy.

Differentiation is the process of matching learning targets, tasks, activities, resources and learning support to individuals' needs, styles and rates of learning. In practice, this means it takes a number of forms – content, outcome, resource, task, support and response – within an overall framework:

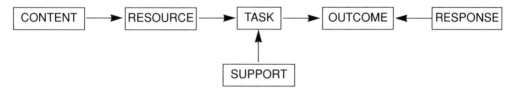

As Dickinson and Wright (1993) point out, pupils' *outcomes* vary and it is your *response* to them that will help differentiation take place. The National Curriculum and GCSE largely prescribe the *content* of pupils' work. But to teach it, *resources* are necessary which should be appropriately pitched. *Tasks* should be provided that help pupils gain knowledge, understanding and skills – and your *support* is essential in assisting pupils through this process.

Differentiation by content

In the days before the National Curriculum, teachers had greater opportunity to differentiate in terms of subject content. Now, curriculum content is largely set down externally by programmes of study and GCSE syllabi. In any case, differentiating by content can often constitute a deprivation model, running counter to the notion of a broad and balanced entitlement. The challenge for schools is to offer an entitlement curriculum *for all* that allows access by pupils at different levels.

Differentiation by outcome

This involves the same general tasks being required of all pupils. As Spillman (1991) notes, you will find it is most effective where the stimulus is lively and questions are open-ended and flexible enough to allow children to respond at their individual levels in terms of style, length and complexity. For example:

- in PE, pupils could devise a gymnastic sequence to include a variety of balance and flight movements, with a range of skills being displayed;
- in History, pupils could be shown various sources about the execution of King Charles I and then asked to produce their own account.

The implication for you, as a new teacher, is that you must ensure questions, activities and resources are accessible to *all* children, with a genuine hierarchy of valid answers stretching from the simple to the sophisticated. The fact that a task generates a range of answers does not, in itself, mean it has been successful in causing pupils to make the optimum level of progress. For instance, the language of the exercise might not be very accessible to less able pupils. On the other hand, reliance on common questions is likely to limit the challenges available for high attainers.

Differentiation by resource

One way you can differentiate with your resources is to match the *readability* of textbooks to children's reading ages in order to ascertain their suitability. Word analyses, where there are more than three syllables (e.g. 'differentiation'!), give some indication of semantic difficulties. Analyses of sentence length provide an idea of the complex relationship of ideas introduced in the text. Use tests for measuring gobbledygook, e.g. the *Flesch Reading Ease Score* or the *Cloze Procedure*.

It is also important to match *worksheets and other resources* to pupils' ability levels. A mismatch will frustrate youngsters at either end of the spectrum. Powell (1991) and Dickinson (1996) both identify many important factors, including:

- design and layout, so that the page is not cluttered;
- accessibility of language;
- use of specialist terminology, so long as words are explained;
- inclusion of relevant illustrations to aid explanation and recall;
- structuring text under sub-headings to help pupils work through documents.

If line length is too long, readers will scan rather than read carefully. Emphases should be in bold rather than upper case, as poor readers find lower case easier to handle (except dyslexics). Difficult readers find ragged text easier to follow than justified. The availability of desktop publishing means there is no longer any reason for teachers' resources to resemble ransom notes culled from newspaper headlines!

The production of *study guides*, covering a module or topic of work, is valuable in helping pupils to make use of differentiated resource materials and to undertake differentiated activities. Encouraging the use of resources does require a well-managed storage and retrieval system. Study guides are a suitable means of embodying study skills into modules of work in order to ensure they are not taught in the manner of the waterless method of swimming instruction! They are particularly necessary where self-access learning is being encouraged, in which you will assume the role of facilitator and counsellor in the learning process.

The provision of *specialised resources* can be valuable for alternative work in practical subjects. In PE, for instance, there is equipment like low impact hockey balls, plastic cricket bats or flotation swimming aids.

✎ **Activity 5.2**
Choose four 100-word extracts from different sections of a book you use with a class. To calculate the Reading Ease Score, you must:

- *count the number of syllables (treat numbers as single words)*
- *count the number of sentences*

- *work out the average number of syllables per 100 words (A)*
- *work out the average number of words per sentence (B)*
- *then calculate this formula: 206.835 – (0.846 x A) – (1.015 x B)*
- *now match the answer from your calculation to a reading age*

Flesch formula score	Reading age
90–100	10
80–90	11
70–80	12
60–70	13–14
50–60	15–17
30–50	18–21
0–30	Genius!

✎ Activity 5.3

Gather together a selection of worksheets produced in your department. Analyse each one in the light of criteria such as layout, sub-headings, illustrations and accessibility of language.

Differentiation by task

This method of differentiation involves providing a variety of tasks for pupils at different levels of ability. You can do it by providing pupils with:

- different starting points sequenced from the simple to the complex;
- tasks matched to differing levels of difficulty;
- choice in what they do to develop their different aptitudes and interests.

Scope must be allowed for *individual, paired or group work.* You should encourage pupils to use *different methods of reporting information* – such as letters, advertisements, posters, oral work, diagrams, video and cassette taping, dialogue or drama. All too often we expect children to use the one single medium of formal writing, which can be uninspiring.

One mechanism for identifying differentiated activities is *Bloom's Taxonomy of Thinking Skills* (1956). It provides a helpful framework for pitching activities at specific levels of cognitive complexity. It is also valuable for devising stepped activities with progressively more challenging concepts (see boxed text overleaf).

Schemes of work provided by your department should reflect differentiated provision, by identifying upper and lower ability reinforcements and extensions for a common core. Spillman (1991) sees it working as follows. All pupils share the common learning experiences. Opportunities are then provided for children to re-learn key concepts, skills and content, while the extensions prompt them to develop higher order skills or use additional material.

It is possible that you might wish to use the opportunity offered by *extracurricular time* to do further enrichment work, e.g. sports and musical activities and writing clubs.

Differentiation by support and resource

It is right and proper to provide means of support for pupils in any learning situation. There are various ways that you can help to do this, such as:

- individual support where learning needs are diagnosed, e.g. going through work, questioning, offering suggestions;
- using support staff, parents, or other pupils in the class;

A topic on Food based on Bloom's Taxonomy

Knowledge...
Name the four main groups of food.
Collect pictures of fruits and vegetables. Label them and name your favourite.

Comprehension...
Compare two green vegetables – their shape, size, taste and how they grow.
Cut out pictures from magazines or draw them to make a breakfast, lunch and dinner. Find out how many calories these foods contain.

Application...
Make a collage of foods you like to eat.
Sow a large vegetable seed, watch it grow and draw the stages of its growth.

Analysis...
List all the things that a cow gives us.
Make a crossword puzzle of tasty fruits. Give good clues.

Synthesis...
Make up your own recipe for a really nutritious cake.

Evaluate...
Work out how nutritious your dinner was last night.
An apple a day keeps the doctor away. What does this saying mean?

- making additional resources available, e.g. reference books, dictionaries, the school library, the Internet, CD–ROMs, scanners;
- team teaching, which facilitates lead lessons, individual tuition and group work;
- small-group tutoring after a whole-class introduction;
- pupils reviewing each other's work or even 'pairing' pupils in order to coach each other;
- ensuring *all* levels of achievement are recognised and celebrated.

The last point emphasises the value of responding to pupils' individual achievements. In many cases, improvements in the quality of their work will be modest and gradual. It is important, therefore, to acknowledge a pupil's work based on his/her past achievements. By doing this, you can ensure everyone develops a positive feeling of achievement, no matter how modest. Remember Tim Brighouse's statement that achievement is all about improving on where you were *yesterday*.

Making differentiated responses to pupils involves recognising and rewarding achievement – and then getting them to do better next time. This philosophy underpins good practice in marking and report writing. Yet OFSTED's report on urban education (1993) criticised schools for not sufficiently creating opportunities for setting individual targets. By actually doing this, you can encourage children to challenge and push themselves fully.

✎ Activity 5.4
Select a topic for one of the classes you teach. Then consider how best to plan its delivery in terms of:

- identifying different ways the topic might be presented to pupils
- devising relevant tasks within the topic
- selecting appropriate tasks for particular pupils
- anticipating the possible responses by pupils
- preparing a suitable way of assessing the work.

How classroom management can help differentiation

Differentiation by resource, task, support and response all have major implications for classroom management and teacher time, given the strains and stresses caused by 'initiative-overload' and the necessity to reconcile competing priorities for one's time and energy. The following points, included in a teachers' pack devised by Powell and Dickinson (n.d.), are good practice for you to implement.

Good class teaching – This should motivate and enthuse your pupils, generate intellectual curiosity, consolidate their previous learning, and get them involved through questioning, paired and group work. It will help you to create time to support individuals and groups via productive dialogue if less time is spent on clarifying tasks and responding to interruptions.

Agreed procedures – These should cover points such as how to enter the classroom, paying attention to the teacher, listening to and respecting each other's viewpoints, movement around the room, use of resources, expectations about class and homework, and responsibility roles for resources. Ground rules will create a climate in which pupils of different abilities develop the confidence to express themselves without fear of ridicule.

Group activities – The value of this type of work is to make lessons participative, thereby encouraging children to be more confident about asking questions and taking on more challenges. Pupils do not always take part successfully in group discussions, presentations and role-play, so you may need to develop collaborative work styles through planned stages.

Examples of techniques advocated by Waterhouse (1990) include:
- *Snowballing* – Individuals brainstorm thoughts on an issue, which they share with a partner. Each pair then reports to a group to reach a team consensus.
- *Reviewing* – Start a lesson with a review of the previous lesson. Do it in groups without the teacher in order to avoid a 'dependency' mentality.
- *Hot seating* – Individuals or groups role-play a character under study. Others then pose questions for the ones in the hot seats to answer.

Organising resources – Differentiation can be made more manageable by ensuring resources are easily accessible. Numbering or labelling or colour coding, familiarising pupils with the retrieval system and making storage space a priority are ways to do this.

Manageable recording – There is likely to be a monitoring burden for you if pupils are working on different tasks, concentrating on different personal targets and using different resources. Therefore, you should think about developing systems that let pupils do some of the recording themselves. It will also help increase their understanding of assessment criteria.

Layout of furniture – In order to manage a range of resources and activities and find time to support pupils, you should think carefully about your classroom organisation. There is a range of possibilities for the organisation of desks and chairs to support teacher-led activities; individual, paired or group activities; common, separate or circus activities; team teaching; etc.

It is important that you understand these approaches are not mutually exclusive – it is a matter of where you place the emphasis. You will find it productive to employ different emphases with different children on different occasions. No single blueprint will work in all situations. Some of the suggested approaches can be implemented quickly, while others involve the production of different tasks and resources that can be more time-consuming. Very often, what you attempt depends on what you find most manageable or familiar, although such decisions should also reflect the different needs of your pupils.

References

Bloom, B. (1956) *Taxonomy of Educational Objectives.* London: Longman.

DES (1989) *Discipline in Schools. Report of the Committee of Enquiry Chaired by Lord Elton.* London: HMSO/DES.

Dickinson, C. (1996) *Effective Learning Activities.* Stafford: Network Educational Press.

Dickinson, C. and Wright, J. (1993) *Differentiation: A Practical Handbook of Classroom Strategies.* Coventry: NCET.

OFSTED (1993) *Access and Achievement in Urban Education.* London: HMSO.

Powell, R. (1991) *Resources for Flexible Learning.* Stafford: Network Educational Press.

Powell, R. and Dickinson, C. (n.d.) *Classroom Management.* Stafford: Network Educational Press.

Spillman, J. (1991) 'Decoding Differentiation', *Special Children* **44**.

Stradling, B. and Saunders, L (1993) 'Differentiation in practice: responding to the needs of all pupils', *Educational Research* **35**(2), 127–32.

Visser, J. (1993) *Differentiation: Making It Work.* Stafford: NASEN Publications.

Waterhouse, P. (1990) *Classroom Management.* Stafford: Network Educational Press.

Chapter 6
Teaching for effective learning

The most successful improvements in school performance have come about where there is a clear focus on what should be the cardinal priority: teaching and learning. This vision facilitates the 'critical interventions' in pupils' classroom experiences which, as Tim Brighouse argues, are likely to enhance their academic performance. In schools, we are at a point now where our collective knowledge is such that we can confidently identify teaching methods that promote effective learning.

The previous chapter dealt with a variety of teaching styles within the context of differentiation. This one examines what constitutes effective classroom *learning*, so that NQT readers can gain some ideas about adapting and developing their teaching styles in ways that respond to their pupils' different learning needs. In discussing this important interface, three essential points are explored:

1. Defining 'learning'
2. How children learn
3. Promoting self-esteem in the young learner

Defining 'learning'

Kyriacou (1986) explains learning in terms of 'a change in pupils' behaviour which takes place as a result of being engaged in an educational experience'. NQTs, and all other teachers, have a responsibility to present their subject knowledge, skills and understanding in ways that help children learn. You will develop competence in this from anecdotal conversations with colleagues, observing others teach and reflecting critically on your own work. As your experience grows, it will give you the confidence to employ a repertoire of teaching styles that influence positively pupils' learning outcomes.

Pupils learn in various ways, so you need to appreciate the elements that make up basic learning processes and how these differ from one child to another. The best known analysis of learning styles is derived from the work of Kolb (1984), and Honey and Mumford (1986). They identify four broad learning styles, which will change over time and according to context:

- *reflector* – learning by feeling and through experience;
- *theorist* – learning by watching: ideas are important;
- *pragmatist* – learning by thinking: enjoys problem-solving;
- *activist* – learning by doing.

On the basis of this analysis, Dickinson (1996) identifies a variety of activities that can be employed by teachers to support the four different types of learner (see Table 6.1).

Table 6.1 Types of learner

Activist	Reflector
Favourite question: If? *Strengths: Action, carrying out plans.* *Goal: To make things happen.* Open-ended, problem-solving, group work. Dramatic play. Broad brief with choices. Presentations. Work in a variety of contexts. Opportunities to make mistakes.	*Favourite question: Why?* *Strengths: Innovation and imagination.* *Goal: Self-involvement in issues.* Debate and conversations. Action planning. Structured group work. Peer teaching and learning. Reflecting on performance/target setting. Practical work. Comprehension exercises which encourage speculation. Opportunities to hypothesise, ask questions, use imagination.
Pragmatist	**Theorist**
Favourite question: How does this work? *Strengths: Practical application of ideas.* *Goal: To bring view of present into line with future security.* Problem-solving. Mentoring. Role-playing. Field trips. Making and constructing. Wide variety of media. Variety of note-taking templates.	*Favourite question: What?* *Strengths: Creating concepts.* *Goal: Self-satisfaction and intellectual recognition.* Investigations. Reading. Guest speakers. Use of library/factual research. Lectures. Essay writing. Puzzles. Coursework. Use of conceptual models. Tests.

(Dickinson 1996, pp. 52–3)

Bowring-Carr and West-Burnham (1997) point to the ways in which a diagnosis of preferred learning styles can help the learner, namely:

- identification of optimum learning circumstance;
- avoidance of inappropriate learning situations;
- development of alternative strategies;
- relating a learning need to a learning style.

Just as pupils have a preferred style of learning, so teachers are inclined to teach in a particular way, possibly without thinking about it. Bowring-Carr and West-Burnham point out the obvious implication: in the absence of a diagnosis of preferred learning styles, there could well be a mismatch with the teacher's delivery of the lesson. Swimming against the tide of a pupil's favoured style could fetter progress, with worrying repercussions for his/her involvement in, and benefit from, the learning experience. Children's capacity to learn, they note, is often the result of 'an interpretive relationship between teacher and learner'. That relationship is destined to succeed only if there are shared constructs between teacher and learners.

Gagné (1985) has pointed to five main areas that contribute to pupil learning:

- *verbal information* – knowing facts, names, principles and generalisations;
- *intellectual skills* – knowing how, rather than knowing that;
- *cognitive strategies* – thinking, memorising, dealing with novel situations;
- *attitudes* – emotions which influence personal action;
- *motor skills* – physical tasks, e.g. playing an instrument.

Another important consideration if learning is to occur is that you must find out and take into account *what pupils already know*. The learning process has to start from where the learner is and how he/she got there. Where this is not done, as Gardner (1993) observes, school work is found to be difficult and pointless, with a potential collision between forms of knowledge and understanding offered by the school and those already absorbed by the pupil outside the scholastic environment.

Any learning opportunities that seek to address this reality must involve certain approaches that necessitate you behaving more as a 'learning manager'. It will have implications for your ability to get through the quantity of material that burdens so many programmes of study and exam syllabi. Nonetheless, the following factors, based on Capel *et al.* (1995) are important:

- ascertaining the prior *knowledge* that the child has so the necessary links can be made with what is currently being taught;
- finding out what *meanings and concepts* the pupil has generated already from their background, attitudes and experiences;
- identifying the pupil's *skills* and planning the lesson from that starting point;
- investigating a child's *points of view* and then stimulating him/her to reconsider or modify such opinions.

✎ Activity 6.1

1. Recall some past experience of learning – either as a pupil or at university or on a course – that was bad. Then do the same for a good experience. What made these features good and bad?

2. Think about a subject you are about to teach and identify the knowledge, concepts and skills that you expect to develop. Then make a comparable list relating to the *prior* knowledge, concepts and skills you expect your pupils to have picked up from previous teachers and from their everyday social and intuitive learning.

How children learn

On to a brief consideration of some theories of learning. Teachers tend to be distrustful of theories – they prefer practical applications, or 'tips for teachers' about everything. Nevertheless, theories provide frameworks for an analysis of learning situations and a language to describe the learning that is taking place. They offer different views of what pupils are like, what knowledge is and how it develops.

Jean Piaget

Piaget (1962) argued that child development progresses through several stages, each of which has underlying mental structures. Young children's thinking relies mainly on concrete operations – in other words, everyday experience and intuition shapes them. But as they get older, children can increasingly absorb abstract concepts until, in adolescence, they reach formal operational thinking. They are then ready to use forms of logical and rational reasoning. Putting Piaget's theory in the context of the classroom leads to the concept of 'readiness' – that is, it is only when children's classroom experiences correlate with their evolving stage of understanding that they learn effectively. So by using Piagetian ideas to examine the intellectual demand in curriculum content, teachers can judge how appropriate they are for pupils of a specific age and ability.

However, you should be wary of blanket labels. One key task is to set work for pupils in which they can experience success and yet be given opportunities for stretching their minds. Research shows that difficult ideas can be taught to pupils if pitched at an appropriate level, thereby accelerating their cognitive development. So what teachers need to do is find ways of encouraging higher-order thinking skills. One way is to use Bloom's Taxonomy of Thinking Skills (see Chapter 5 'Differentiation and effective teaching') as a framework for setting questions and activities at increasingly demanding levels, relating to knowledge, comprehension, application, analysis, synthesis and evaluation.

L S Vygotsky

Vygotsky (1962) emphasised learning through teaching and activity. Intelligence is influenced by a capacity for being instructed, as well as for learning. Communication, social experiences and interpersonal relationships, therefore, play a vital role. He coined the notion of a zone of proximal development, i.e. the gap between what a pupil is able to do alone and what he/she can achieve with the guidance offered by a teacher. The implication for classroom learning is that you need to give children opportunities to move from their current level of development by making sure they fully grasp what is taught, preferably by involving them in their learning as far as possible. As Vygotsky put it, 'What a child can do today in cooperation [with a more knowledgeable person], tomorrow he will be able to do on his own'.

J S Bruner

Bruner (1966) put emphasis on the importance of 'information processing' in helping learning take place. Key inputs in developing children's knowledge, skills and understanding are language, communication and teaching. What they enable the learner to do is look for patterns, regularity and predictability, with the teacher acting the part of learning assistant in this process. One point made by Bruner is that learning can be assisted by the individual's proficiency in using interactive aids to learning, such as computers. Effective teaching also involves showing pupils how to *apply* knowledge in different situations and reason their way through things for themselves. Exploring inter-relationships and spotting connections are two obvious outcomes.

Roger Sperry

In the context of mental development, it is worth noting Sperry's research in the USA on the two hemispheres of the brain and the way both have specialised functions. Scans of electrical activity on the two sides show:

- the left-hand side is better at solving mathematical problems or putting information in sequence;
- the right-hand side is better at recognising images, detecting patterns and synthesising information.

It is said that individuals tend to favour activity on one side or the other. There is a gender dimension, too, in that females tend to be more analytical/reflective because that part of the brain is more highly developed, whereas males are more speculative and experiential. The implication for teaching and learning is that one should try to involve pupils in activities that develop *both* sides of the brain, especially areas in which they might be weak. A 'whole-brain' approach will get children using functions from both sides and access all the senses, thereby improving their all round mental performance. Smith (1996) represents the dichotomy as shown in Table 6.2.

Table 6.2 Specialised brain functions

Left brain	Right brain
Language	Forms and patterns
Logic	Spatial manipulation
Mathematical formulae	Rhythm
Number	Musical appreciation
Sequence	Images and pictures
Linearity	Dimension
Analysis	Imagination
Words of a song	Tune of song
Learning from the part to the whole	Learns the whole first, then parts
Phonetic reading system	Daydreaming and visioning
Unrelated factual information	Whole language reader
	Relationships in learning

(Smith 1996, p. 20)

Howard Gardner

Gardner (1983) is one of the newest significant writers in this field, having done ground-breaking work in the fields of neurology and cognitive psychology regarding our ability to work intelligently. He argues there are seven types of preference for learning, which he calls *multiple intelligences*, rather than one monolithic IQ (see Table 6.3). Each ability/skill/talent is directly related to a particular area of the brain. Most learners will have an uneven profile, in that they will be high in some areas and low in others. It is not a new idea: in 1949 the philosopher Gilbert Ryle claimed that 'the boxer, the surgeon, the poet and the salesman' each possess their own kinds of intelligence.

The implication for learning is clear. Schools should use teaching methods, offer learning activities, design tasks and projects, devise assessments, produce resources and equip classrooms to enable teachers to work through, and aim at, all these intelligences with pupils – not just the first two traditional ones based on linguistic and mathematical prowess. Smith (1996) notes that the intrapersonal type is one that schools neglect the most. Also, bodily, musical and spatial intelligences have fewer formal opportunities for expression unless schools encourage the creative and performing arts side of the curriculum.

Gardner thinks that virtually any topic can be approached in a number of ways, thus opening up effective learning to the largest range of pupils. Two key questions for you to reflect on are:

- am I sufficiently confident to offer a wide variety of opportunities for children to access the different intelligences?
- does it matter if some pupils have explored a topic thoroughly through other forms of expression that do not necessarily involve formal written work?

Table 6.3 Multiple intelligences

Intelligences	Characteristics	Examples
Verbal-linguistic	Speaking and writing, especially at a conceptual level.	A verbal explanation or e-mailing a report to someone else or telling a story. Puns and poems. Listening, writing, reading and discussion.
Logical-mathematical	Deductive and inductive reasoning, calculating and logical thinking.	A code-breaking game or syllogism or work with number, patterns, measurement and estimation.
Visual-spatial	Painting, drawing and sculpting, including thinking in 3 dimensions.	A mind map to link causes of an historical event or an architectural design or creating a display. Producing graphs and maps.
Bodily-kinaesthetic	Using hands and body in expressive mode; good control of objects.	Role-play or dance sequence involving coordinated responses. Energisers and educational visits.
Musical	Composing, playing an instrument, singing, enjoys rhythm.	A set of historical dates, mathematical formulae or the periodic table rapped or sung to a powerful beat. Poems and jingles.
Interpersonal	Interacting with, understanding and relating to others.	A discussion or paired/group activities or looking at issues from different perspectives. Collaborative learning exercises. Interviews.
Intrapersonal	Self-awareness and motivation, and understanding personal potential.	An individual action plan or encouraging exploration and sharing of feelings or opportunities for self-reflection.

Richard Perkins

Finally, mention should be made of another radical view of intelligence. Perkins (1995) defines three types of intelligence:

- *neural* – which is strongly influenced by inheritance;
- *experimental* – which results from the development of expertise in a given field;
- *reflective* – strategies and attitudes which make better use of one's mind.

The encouraging feature of experimental intelligence is that, given the right attitude on the part of pupils, it is learnable. The same applies to reflective intelligence. Teachers can show pupils ways to make more productive use of their minds and enhance their thinking process by strategies like memorising, problem-solving, reasoning and devising imaginative responses.

> ✎ **Activity 6.2**
> Discuss with your induction tutor some of the practical classroom applications of these ideas about how pupils learn.
> For example, you could consider case studies of individual pupils in relation to Gardner's multiple intelligences in order to identify the best learning strategies to use with them.
> Alternatively, you could devise short lesson plans based upon presenting pupils with a range of activities associated with each of the intelligences – what Lazear calls a 'multiple intelligences toolbox'.

Promoting self-esteem in the young learner

Effective learning arises from making children active partners in the process of learning – in other words, providing them with a sense of value and purpose, ownership and personal involvement about what they do in the classroom. At its root is the need to nurture in pupils feelings of positive self-esteem and belief in themselves. Without this vital ingredient, ideas about effective learning will lack impact.

Smith (1996) offers a comprehensive strategy whereby teachers can reinforce pupils' motivation and commitment using the *BASIS* approach – an acronym for *Belonging, Aspirations, Safety, Identity* and *Success*. Substantially summarised, the BASIS approach is shown in Table 6.4.

Table 6.4 The BASIS approach

Belonging	Pupils with a sense of belonging feel they are part of a class that is important to them, whereas children with limited skills in this area demonstrate negative behaviour, e.g. bullying, showing off.
Methods	• *Involve pupils in paired and group activities to encourage cooperative learning and build team skills* • *Emphasise the collaborative achievements of the class and the contribution that individuals make*
Aspirations	Pupils need to believe learning has a purpose. A lack of aspiration leads to negativity. So offer plenty of motivation and set realistic goals.
Methods	• *Provide exercises where pupils make decisions* • *Teach ways of solving problems, e.g. flow charts* • *Use role models from the pupils' own experiences* • *Identify successes in past performance and build on them* • *Relate tasks to goals and action plan with pupils*
Safety	Pupils feel comfortable in a group where there are expectations and ground rules. Where there is learner security, they will be more willing to take risks.
Methods	• *Apply school and classroom rules fairly and consistently* • *Use a behaviour and reward policy* • *Avoid put-downs* • *Get to know pupils in contexts outside the classroom*
Identity	If pupils know their strengths as well as weaknesses, it prevents disillusionment, sensitivity to criticism or reluctance to participate.
Methods	• *Give frequent constructive and honest feedback* • *Develop one-to-one tutoring and action planning*

	• Say something positive about, and to, every pupil in the class • Give pupils opportunities to express their feelings
Success *Methods*	Regularly affirming success – however modest – reinforces the belief that new challenges can be met. Otherwise pupils will not take risks or offer ideas. • *Teach active listening skills to help feedback* • *Find areas of success and promote them* • *When pupils do well, refer them to heads of department/year heads/senior staff* • *Discourage comparisons with other pupils' work* • *Break down steps to improvement into small chunks* • *Give pupils opportunities to talk about their interests* • *Show pupils how destructive negative self-talk can be*

(Smith 1996, pp. 27–30)

This chapter represents no more than an introduction to a few of the fundamental theories and issues relating to how and why children learn. There is much more that could be written about practical methods of active learning that encourage pupils to be more methodical and organised in their approach. Other factors – like the layout of the classroom furniture and displays – also contribute to creating an effective learning environment. Table 6.5 lists just a few examples of techniques – not in any order of priority – which you could employ, based on suggestions made by Smith (1996).

Table 6.5 Active learning techniques

Chained review	Group work on a topic. Present separate sections to each other in turn.
Concept mapping	Main theme in centre, with subsidiary ideas feeding out, then further points from them in turn. Use lines/arrows for connections. Activates patterning capacity of brain and establishes connections between facts/ideas.
Get a partner	Work in pairs or with partner – listening, testing, interrogating.
Just a minute	Once pupils have listened to teacher's talk or completed a piece of reading/writing, get individuals to give one-minute talk without pausing.
Mnemonics	Good technique for memorising categories or lists.
Mobile torture	Sit in a circle. Teacher starts questioning pupils in order of seating. Failure to answer means pupil moves to next 'hot' seat . . . and so on till a correct answer is given.
Paired review	In pairs, describe to each other three key things/most important points/most useful information learned.
Posters	Visually summarise important content with colourful posters. Use old wallpaper rolls. Ideal for group revision and concept mapping.
Raps, rhythm or rhyme	Put something in verse – easier to remember. Good for dates, kings/queens, lists of facts.
Review to music	Useful for generating calm, supportive ambience when working. Music with 60-70 beats per minute is especially good. Volume should be only just perceptible.
Self-questioning	Encourage pupils working on new topics to ask: • What are the key points? • How well do I understand it? • How might I explain it to somebody else?

Skim and speed reading	Scan down a page for key points, then go back and read thoroughly.
Visualisation	Visualise key names/facts/concepts in bright, colourful images.
Yes/No	In pairs, one pupil asks a series of quick-fire questions about topics. Aim is to persuade partner to answer yes/no. Partner's aim is to give explanation rather than one-word answer.

(Smith 1996, pp. 81–8)

The key point is that the teacher's role is to facilitate learning: it is not enough for pupils simply to acquire facts. If theories of learning are to have a beneficial impact on children's learning, their classroom experience should:

• allow them to enquire and pose problems;
• provide them with a stimulating learning environment;
• assist them in making independent discoveries.

Teachers can do everything in their power to empower and motivate children to learn, but cannot do the learning for them. Pupils must be encouraged to be purposeful, rather than passive, and ultimately be responsible for their own learning. It becomes a process, therefore, in which the interaction of the teacher and the taught determines the quality of the learning that takes place.

References

Bowring-Carr, C. and West-Burnham, J. (1997) *Effective Learning in Schools*. London: Pitman.

Bruner, J. (1966) *The Process of Education*. New York: Vintage.

Capel, S., Leask, M. and Turner, T. (1995) *Learning to Teach in the Secondary School*. London: Routledge.

Dickinson, C. (1996) *Effective Learning Activities*. Stafford: Network Educational Press.

Gagné, R. (1985) *The Conditions of Learning and Theory of Instruction*. New York: Holt, Rinehart & Winston.

Gardner, H. (1983) *Frames of Mind*. London: Fontana.

Gardner, H. (1993) *The Unschooled Mind*. London: Fontana.

Honey, P. and Mumford, P. (1986) *A Manual of Learning Styles*. Maidenhead: Peter Honey.

Kolb, D. (1984) *Experiential Learning: Experience as the Source of Learning and Development*. Englewood Cliffs, NJ: Prentice-Hall.

Kyriacou, C. (1986) *Effective Teaching in Schools*. Hemel Hempstead: Simon & Schuster.

Perkins, D. (1995) *Outsmarting IQ: The Emerging Science of Learnable Intelligence*. New York: Free Press.

Piaget, J. (1962) *Judgement and Reasoning in the Child*. London: Routledge and Kegan Paul.

Smith, A. (1996) *Accelerated Learning in the Classroom*. Stafford: Network Educational Press.

Vygotsky, L. (1962) *Thought and Language*. Cambridge, Mass.: MIT Press.

Chapter 7

Assessment, recording and reporting

Assessment, recording and reporting are an integral part of any good teacher's repertoire of professional practice. Newly qualified teachers will find assessment takes place informally through their expertise, observational skills and intuition. These initial impressions are then confirmed or modified by a variety of school-based measures and external tests and examinations. Finally, the accumulated evidence of pupils' attainments is recorded and reported to parents.

The pace of curriculum change – from GCSE to the National Curriculum, from ROA to GNVQ, and now the new post-16 reforms – has generated considerable change in assessment practice. These influences – coupled with issues of devolved school management and parental choice – have contributed to the increasing public accountability schools face. Consequently, assessment issues are in the forefront of educational thinking and parental concern. No new teacher can afford to ignore them!

Definitions of assessment

[The] wide range of methods for evaluating pupil performance and attainment, including formal testing and examinations, practical and oral assessment, classroom-based assessment carried out by teachers and portfolios.

(Gipps 1994, p. vii)

The judgement teachers make about a child's attainment based on knowledge gained through techniques such as observation, questioning, marking pieces of work and testing.

(Dearing 1994, p. 102)

Definitions of assessment are legion. Essentially, it deals with any evaluative observation or measurement of individual pupils or groups of pupils. Knowledge and understanding of the different forms of assessment – and the ability to employ them effectively – are essential professional skills for any new teacher. You will have been introduced to assessment in your own subjects during initial teacher training.

This chapter focuses on several key whole-school aspects of this subject that should serve to underpin your measurement and evaluation of pupils' learning, namely:

1. The purposes of assessment
2. Modes of assessment
3. Reliability and validity
4. Effective marking
5. Examples of good assessment practice
6. Recording pupil achievement
7. Reporting to parents.

The purposes of assessment

Assessment has various purposes. Those summarised here are not mutually exclusive, as there is considerable overlap when translated into practice:

- to gather data about each child's progress and identify individual needs;
- to place pupils in appropriate teaching sets, identify the different needs of pupils in mixed ability sets, and inform subject choices at KS4 and post-16;
- to monitor teaching standards and ensure learning objectives are met;
- to inform future curriculum planning;
- to provide pupils with an incentive for learning by involving them in assessment and providing specific feedback on strengths and weaknesses;
- to report accurately to parents on progress, attitude and attainment;
- to provide information for governors, employers, FE, HE, the LEA, the DfEE, the QCA and OFSTED;
- to fulfil statutory obligations to assess, record and report pupils' progress in National Curriculum subjects;
- to meet the requirements of public exam courses regarding coursework, making tiered exam entries and predicting future performance.

From all these purposes, Gipps and Murphy (1994) pinpoint two broad categories:

- *pupil-centred purposes* relating to diagnosis, evaluation and guidance, which support the teaching-learning process;
- *teacher-centred purposes* to do with prediction, selection, certification, placement and evaluation of the curriculum.

Publication of league tables of school test and exam results has emphasised the latter category of 'high stakes' assessment, to the detriment of the former category's diagnostic role.

✎ Activity 7.1
How were *you* assessed, either at school or university? Think of some examples of both encouraging and dispiriting experiences at the hands of your teachers or tutors. What was it about each of them that you found particularly positive or negative? How are these experiences going to influence ways in which you act as an assessor of pupils' work and effort nowadays?

✎ Activity 7.2
Consider the above list of purposes and then carry out these two exercises:

- place each purpose in one of two categories – *formative* or *summative* – while bearing in mind that some may belong in both categories
- identify the *different audiences* that these purposes are intended to serve (e.g. pupils, parents, employers).

The antagonisms in educational assessment are not new. By setting the debate within socio-political trends, one can see how in the socially optimistic 1950s and 1960s it concerned itself mainly with access and opportunity. Our expanding economy promoted confidence in various forms of state welfarism, including education. Then with the slowing of growth in the late 1960s and early 1970s, blame for our structural economic decline was partly laid at education's door. The Callaghan Government called for an improvement in standards to make Britain more competitive and to rejuvenate the economy.

Growing public and media pressure to hold schools accountable for standards of pupil achievement fed into the debate. In the 1980s, as Mrs Thatcher sought greater governmental influence over education, attainment in core subjects was criticised and calls made for the publication of exam results. Thus, 'two cultures' of assessment emerged, one professional and the other managerial.

Modes of assessment

Assessments can be categorised into *formative* and *summative* functions, too.

Formative assessment will involve you continuously assessing pupils' work as an integral part of teaching and learning. Judgements arise through observing how pupils respond to tasks. They are diagnostic, in that they help the child identify strengths and weaknesses so that learning objectives may be more readily achieved. Motivation, guidance and feedback are the outcomes. As Gipps and Murphy (1994) put it, the aim is to help rather than sentence the individual. This type of assessment counterbalances the current benchmark testing of 7, 11 and 14-year-olds.

Where you want to inform others about pupils' attainments, *summative assessment* methods are appropriate. These help you sum up a pupil's progress and take the form of oral/written tests, annual exams, end-of-key stage tests and public exams. Such one-off assessments have the potential to ascertain what pupils know, understand and can do against specified criteria *or* against each other (*criterion-referenced* or *norm-referenced* assessment). The downside is that an over-emphasis on testing encourages competition rather than personal improvement. In particular, it suggests to pupils with low attainments that they lack 'ability', with the result that they believe themselves incapable of learning.

Labour urged to ease off testing

Every pupil's GCSE results could be boosted by one or two grades if there was less emphasis on tests and more on involving young people in their learning. A group of eminent academics today called on the Government to champion pupil-centred 'assessment for learning', or formative assessment...They say there is no evidence testing raises standards. But changing teachers' use of assessment and giving students constructive feedback does...

(*TES*, 3 September 1999)

Exam obsession damages pupils

One of the things I enjoyed most about being an English teacher was watching pupils improve over their two-year, 100 per cent coursework GCSE. So many were a testimony to the power of formative assessment, particularly the disaffected boys, who were increasingly falling through the net. Pupils had to make an effort to meet their assignment deadlines, rather than deferring performance to the exam...We need official recognition of what a pupil has achieved in school, but ample evidence suggests that, the more we test, the more we restrict that achievement.

(Marshall 1999, p. 15)

Black (1998) argues that a review of research literature published since 1986 shows children make significant learning gains where the practice of formative assessments is strengthened. Another important outcome is that improved formative assessment particularly helps low attainers, thus reducing the spread of attainment while also raising it overall. This is important for all new teachers to understand: any 'tail' of low educational achievement is a waste of talent. Furthermore, pupils who see themselves as unable to learn usually end up being disruptive.

You should seek a variety of openings, therefore, to assess pupils in a formative way. Table 7.1 provides some examples of learning activities that present suitable assessment opportunities.

Table 7.1 Learning activities as assessments

Oral evidence	Written evidence	Graphic evidence	Products
Questioning	Questionnaires	Diagrams	Models
Listening	Diaries	Sketches	Artefacts
Discussing	Reports	Drawings	Games
Presentations	Essays	Graphs	Photographs
Interviews	Notes	Printouts	
Debates	Stories	Overlays	
Audio recording	Newspaper articles		
Video recording	Scripts		
Role-play	Short answers		
Simulation	Lists		
	Poems		
	Descriptions		

(Capel *et al.* 1995, p. 275)

✎ Activity 7.3

Having looked at the table of learning activities (Table 7.1), reflect on these questions:

- how frequently do you use these activities in your classrooms?
- why are some used less frequently than others?
- how many are likely to present you with potential evidence on which to base assessments?

Reliability and validity

Assessments have imperfections. Gipps and Stobart (1993) feel this is because they are as much to do with the human beings who administer them as the assessments themselves. Many of these shortcomings arise from a failure to satisfy the interdependent technical requirements of reliability and validity.

Where an assessment strategy has *reliability*, it means one should have confidence that assessments are comparable. Standardised tests are designed to minimise all sources of variance – most importantly, the conditions in which the test takes place and the different interpretations or judgements applied by the marker. In other words:

- if a test were given to a pupil on another day, would he/she obtain the same result?
- if marked by different teachers at the same time, would the same score be given?

A perfectly reliable test is impossible to produce because:

- different tests measure different things;
- they measure only part of a course and so vary from year to year;
- pupils give unexpected answers;
- some questions are poorly written;
- pupils lack consistency in their knowledge and understanding from day to day;
- they are affected by extraneous influences;
- teachers' interpretations vary, particularly with creative responses.

Reliability can be maximised by using formal, multiple choice tests processed by an optical mark reader. Where this is inappropriate, greater consistency is achievable by using uniform mark schemes and then employing simple moderation and standardisation procedures.

If an assessment strategy has *validity*, it means one should have confidence that it is assessing what it is intended to assess. To maximise validity, the assessment should closely resemble the pupils' learning experience, in terms of both content and process. Since this involves taking a much broader view of how to measure children's attainment, different kinds of question and activity will help reflect the complexity of this concept. Confining the format of assessments will sacrifice their validity, e.g. how could one assess conversational French or the dramatic irony in *Macbeth* with a 30-minute summative multiple-choice test? Validity is maximised via informal observations, conversations and discussions about classwork, undertaken and recorded by the teacher.

One key aspect of the validity of assessment concerns *gender bias*. Boys and girls are said to interpret and respond to assessment tasks in different ways because of their different experiences, understandings and priorities. There are persistent findings, for instance, that boys do better on multiple-choice tests because they are more confident about deciding whether an item is correct or not, while girls are more concerned with their *relative* rightness/wrongness (Stobart *et al.* 1992). On the other hand, GCSE coursework requiring extended, analytical responses has brought girls (and middle class pupils) considerable advantage (Gipps 1992). It is important, therefore, to offer children a *balance* of tasks.

1999 reading test more boy-friendly

...I suspect that the main reason for the improvement in the boys' scores [in the 1999 KS2 reading SATs] lies in the content and format of the paper... In 1998 pupils had to read an 850-word extract from a story about two children being evacuated from Germany in December 1938.

The main character was a girl; most of the illustrations were of girls, women and a doll. The final pages were an interview with the female author, 38 out of the 50 available marks were based on this passage and included questions such as 'Explain how you think Clara feels when...' Teachers have told me that in 1998 many boys could not get through the story in time, or lost interest, or could not cope with the empathy required to answer questions.

In 1999 the theme...was spiders. The text was printed in much larger type and was illustrated by diagrams and cartoons. Some questions required a more sophisticated level of response but most of the marks were given for factual comprehension...I was therefore not surprised to hear that the boys had done so well.

(Peter Downes. Letter in *TES*, 15 October 1999)

As a new teacher, you need to be aware of the assessment part of the gender and achievement debate. The task is quite a profound one of exploring:

- boys' and girls' expectations and experiences of subjects;
- how these shape their different interests and ways of responding;
- teacher stereotypes and expectations.

> ✎ **Activity 7.4**
> Carry out some research into the range of assessments used by your department. How far do they reflect reliability and/or validity? Which is the more important concept?
> Then undertake observations of a boy and a girl. *Do* they exhibit different learning styles and what types of assessment do they prefer?

Effective marking

Marking is a form of assessment in which another person (usually, but not always, the teacher) responds to a pupil's work. It may be formative or summative. Successful marking should result in some change in pupils' work: either unsatisfactory habits are reduced or more acceptable ones developed. It is *not* a worthwhile activity if the collection of marks to fill up record books is given greater priority than the analysis of pupils' work to discern learning needs.

Research suggests that successful marking has the following characteristics:

- it is an integral part of the learning process and not 'bolted on';
- it is honest, positive and constructive, rather than destructive;
- it enables pupils to assess their work and plan their own learning;
- it provides feedback about progress and indicates future steps;
- it is manageable;
- it operates from known and agreed standards;
- it is read (or heard) and acted upon by pupils;
- it distinguishes between effort and attainment.

At its most successful, marking opens a dialogue with the pupil and should inform future practice by offering guidance on how work can be improved. Unsuccessful marking, or its continued absence, is a powerful demotivator. It also sends distinct messages to parents. You should not undertake marking for its own sake: it should be a meaningful communication between you, as teacher, and your individual pupils. That is why raw marks or grades are of limited value unless clearly placed in context. So written comments and advice are essential. They should be sufficiently frequent to support the pupil and offer guidance on moving forward. Consequently, you need to encourage pupils to read *and act upon* their comments. This is not to downplay the value of speaking directly to a pupil. However, oral comments alone provide no record of advice for either the pupil or teacher concerned.

> **Problems with marking**
> Marking is usually conscientious but often fails to offer guidance on how work can be improved. In a significant minority of cases, marking reinforces under-achievement and under-expectation by being too generous or unfocused. Information about pupil performance received by the teacher is insufficiently used to inform subsequent work.
>
> OFSTED (1996)

Some learners' recollections of how their work was marked

As soon as we get our books back there's a great 'What did you get? I got so-and-so'. If you mark people low they get discouraged and people do care about their marks. If you get an E it's quite a nasty punishment and we have one teacher who says things like 'Somebody who shall remain nameless let our form down by getting only 3 out of 10'. Of course, everyone knows who it is. Why do teachers get us to call out our marks instead of putting them in a book while marking them? *Jane, aged 11.*

My first notion of the change in emphasis between junior and secondary school came when I had to write an essay on Neolithic man for my first piece of History homework. I started 'My name is Wanda and I am the son of the headman in the village'. The History master read it out to the rest of the class in a sarcastic voice. Everybody laughed and I felt deeply humiliated. I got 3/20 for covering the page with writing. I hated History after that until the third year. *Daniel, aged 17.*

A teacher's comments on a 13-year-old's essays in History

10/20   Spelling atrocious.
12/20   Watch your tenses, but getting better.
4/20   Go through this work and put it into the past tense.
4/20   Do your spelling corrections. Very poor work.

Comments by a Geography teacher in the books of 12-year-olds

You work quickly, and I'm very pleased with this and with your interest. Do try to be neater, especially in your diagrams. This would increase your marks. Effort: B+. Attainment: C.

You explain your plans well. You're self-critical in a constructive way in the last section. Good summary of Newcastle's actual plans. Excellent presentation. Effort: A. Attainment: B+.

(Jones 1994)

✎ Activity 7.5

Study the extracts above and then consider the following issues:

* what marking approaches are most/least helpful?
* how do you react to spelling mistakes, poor grammar and punctuation?
* how effective do you think the marks, comments and corrections were in helping the 13-year-old pupil improve?
* what part should discussion with pupils play in improving their work?

Examples of good assessment practice

OFSTED guidelines for the inspection of schools (1995) call for the effective assessment of pupils' attainment and the use of such information in curriculum planning. Fleshing this out, there are several fundamental questions for individual teachers, including those new to the profession, to address:

* Do teachers' assessments relate accurately to National Curriculum requirements?
* How is assessment data used in planning responses to the needs of individual pupils, e.g. those with special educational needs?

- How well are pupils listened and responded to?
- Are their misconceptions recognised and handled?
- How are pupils' responses built on to steer them towards clearer understanding?
- Do the outcomes inform teachers' work and lead to higher standards?
- Do teachers keep accurate and comprehensive achievement records?
- Are samples of work kept which exemplify achievement at different levels?
- Do individual teachers try to ensure comparability in their judgements?
- Are assessment arrangements manageable and economical?
- Do the outcomes assist assessment's various audiences?
- How are pupil records transferred from one teacher to another?

So how can *you*, as an NQT, try to put these OFSTED expectations into practice?

Good practice in reviewing and developing your assessments

- Read and consult your school's policy on assessment. It should be thoroughly absorbed and consistently applied in your teaching.
- Embed assessments in the programmes of study, attainment targets and level descriptions recorded in your departmental schemes of work.
- Establish routines with other teachers for moderating pupils' work at key points. The benefits will be seen in consistency and continuity, improved pupil achievement, and strengthened teacher awareness.
- Don't forget that a regime of 'testing' encourages rote learning.
- Be prepared to use a range of assessment techniques, e.g. observation, flexible questioning, 'eavesdropping', analysis of written and practical work, the use of taped and video evidence.
- Employ talk and questioning, but let your pupils have the chance to answer! Encourage them to discuss their thinking in pairs/groups.
- Make sure the ways you record attainment are accurate, economical and convey the information you need. A 'tick system' may be the most convenient way of noting evidence 'on the hoof' in some situations.
- Assessment should prove useful in establishing the progress pupils make. 'Baseline' processes will measure how much 'value added' progress is subsequently made.
- Ensure your marking is regularly done, consistently applied, in line with school assessment policy, understood by pupils, positive and upbeat about their work, and includes targets for improvement.
- Use assessment data to feed back to pupils, urging them to reflect on and evaluate their work and set targets for themselves.

Self-assessment by pupils

Pupils should be encouraged to engage in self-assessment so they understand the purposes of their work and grasp what they must do to achieve. Children are generally honest in assessing themselves and each other. Indeed, they can be too hard. The main problem you are likely to encounter is that pupils lack a clear picture of the targets their learning is meant to achieve. This is because they often see classroom teaching as an arbitrary sequence of exercises with no overarching rationale.

Therefore, if you are to involve pupils in their own assessment you must realise it requires a modification of the teacher/pupil role and relationship in terms of the following:

- tasks should be justified in respect of learning aims;
- discussions should be used to respond to, and re-orient, pupils' thinking;
- unexpected answers should be rewarded;

- pupils must be encouraged to see assessment as a way of taking greater responsibility for their learning;
- they must be well supported in developing the *skills* of self-evaluation.

Portfolios of exemplary work

Now that Teacher Assessments in most subjects have to be reported to parents, the assessment process should help to make TAs as consistent as possible. Joint planning of assessments, common activities, common mark-schemes and even inter-school moderation are means of doing this.

CASE STUDY

Examples of good assessment practice

In Geography...
individual counselling is given to GCSE pupils throughout their fieldwork project, while departmental record keeping is on a fully computerised basis.

In English...
pupils' folders include self-assessments, exemplar work and report duplicates, while a more formative approach involves pupil–teacher dialogue in lessons and lunchtimes.

In History...
pupils monitor their own progress by recording levels of attainment on 'pupil-speak' record sheets, which increases familiarity with how they are assessed.

In Mathematics...
'Success in Maths' award certificates are given to pupils for good or improving work and senior staff are asked to praise pupils' achievements.

In Modern Languages...
...pupils do self-assessment sheets and then choose tasks suited to their level or aim for the next level once they have consolidated their success.

In Music...
there are practical presentations, which staff assess together on a collaborative basis and they are video or tape-recorded.

In Physical Education...
opportunities are given to pupils to coach and test each other in pairs after instruction from their teacher, with feedback then given to the whole class.

In Religious Education...
revision booklets, exam practice questions and specimen essay answers are used to prepare pupils for the GCSE exam.

In Science...
new record cards have been developed for plotting individual pupils' achievement, effort and progress through Key Stage 3.

In Technology...
a particular skill is selected to focus on in design projects, e.g. designing *or* making, so that assessment does not become unwieldy or contradictory.

(Sneyd Community School, Walsall)

OFSTED has stated that a portfolio approach helps to 'bench-mark' standards. If this is being undertaken successfully in your school, it is likely to involve you contributing to the compilation of a departmental folder of subject work that represents examples of achievement at every level. Teachers' notes and comments will help illustrate levels of attainment. The portfolio should be used in meetings and lessons as a common reference point to help raise the 'level awareness' of both teachers and pupils. Wall displays are another way of communicating such awareness.

Recording pupil achievement

Recording progress and attainment is a vital ingredient of any assessment practice. That is why the DfEE requires schools to keep, as a bare minimum, annually updated records of their pupils' achievements. Decisions about *how* to record assessments are left to individual schools, with the proviso that records should:

- be fit for the purpose they serve and help teachers, senior managers and parents track pupils' progress;
- arise from routine processes of teaching, learning and assessing;
- be manageable, concise and accurate.

OFSTED places particular emphasis on the importance of records in informing the planning of future work and enabling teachers to make judgements about pupils' levels of attainment, especially at the end of a Key Stage. Other functions that you should be aware of include:

- tracking the progress of individual pupils or groups of pupils;
- identifying patterns over time where there are many small steps in pupils' knowledge and skills;
- setting individual and group targets for improvement;
- discussing pupils' progress with their parents and other teachers.

What should be recorded and when?

Teachers' own daily/weekly records	These reflect how far pupils are achieving objectives identified in lesson plans. Teachers routinely observe features of their pupils' learning, but much isn't recorded. Sometimes it helps to annotate lesson plans, e.g. if a concept needs to be returned to.
Teachers' ongoing records	Activities designed to assess pupils' grasp of knowledge and skills often result in written work. Effective marking against specified objectives and a common standard provides a record and feedback to the teacher and pupils. Progress can be reviewed by looking at comments on pupils' work and marks in record books. They can also be used to adjust day-to-day teaching and plan further work. Pupils with IEPs (individual education plans) may have a separate pro forma.
Long-term (termly/ annual) records	Departmental and school assessment records kept for each pupil provide useful data for monitoring progress over a long period. They are also necessary for passing on information to the next teacher. At the end of a Key Stage, the records will need to include statutory test/task results and teacher assessments.

(QCA 1999a, p. 3)

✎ **Activity 7.6**

Choose one of the pupils you teach and ask yourself the following questions:

- how readily can I present a clear picture of the pupil?
- what level of detail am I able to provide?
- how far can I support this information with recorded information?

Reporting to parents

Reports (and meetings with parents) will provide you with the opportunity to review a pupil's progress, discuss strengths and weaknesses, and set targets for the future. Schools are statutorily required to provide one written report to parents each year, although many provide more. Some schools find it useful to stagger the sending out of reports throughout the year, while others use them as end-of-year summative statements.

Some principles of good report writing

Report formats, whether computerised or handwritten, will vary from school to school. However, all will expect you to complete them in an *informative* way. Most parents want to know:

- how their child is performing in relation to their potential and past achievements, to the rest of the class and to any national standards;
- their child's strengths and any particular achievements;
- areas for development and improvement;
- how they can help;
- whether their child is happy, settled and behaving well.

Good reports strive to be *personal to the pupil*. Some evidence suggests parents dislike computer-generated reports when this leads to the production of impersonal statements confined largely to curriculum content. Reports should *communicate clearly*. They should be legibly written, with correct grammar, punctuation and spelling. Comments should be succinct and free of jargon likely to baffle parents.

The report should concentrate on *pupil performance*: what the pupil has or has not learned, rather than what has been taught. It should indicate what standards have been achieved and whether any comparison is being made with previous performance, with other pupils or against national norms. A system of grading for effort and attainment, plus marks or percentages, will help quantify teachers' comments for parents.

Reports can be an important way of *helping pupils make progress*. Highlighting their strengths and recognising achievements in different areas of school life will contribute to this. However, areas for development should be clearly identified and advice given about what steps need to be undertaken to improve. It is important not to obscure low achievement by the use of faint praise or by avoiding mention of a problem. In giving an accurate picture of current attainment, reports should involve the pupil in setting clear, achievable and time-related targets for his or her learning. Even the most able and conscientious pupil can be given suggestions about how to make further progress.

Sample text of part of a Year 9 school report

English Martin has worked well all year. His work on *Romeo and Juliet* showed that he is achieving above average standards in speaking and listening and reading. His drama work showed that he can keep the interest of an audience. Martin needs to improve the quality of his writing, both the length and structure of it as well as his spelling and handwriting. He needs to allow more time for his written work so that he improves the quality by planning more thoroughly and checking his work for spelling errors.

Maths Martin's work is just below the level expected for his age. Although he can add and subtract negative numbers and decimals, he still needs to improve his multiplication and division of whole numbers. He can calculate fractions of parts of quantities and measurements, but has difficulty with percentages. He can make sensible estimates of lengths and angles, but has yet to learn metric and imperial unit equivalents. Martin has a good understanding of graphs and diagrams and interprets them well, drawing sensible conclusions. He has begun to construct pie charts.

Science Martin's attainment is just below the average for his age. Over the last year, the quality of his work has been variable. In biological topics, he has linked his own observations to scientific principles and information from reference books. He has produced particularly good work on small creatures found in the school environment. However, in work related to physical processes he has found it more difficult to link principles to his study. He should think carefully about patterns in what he observes and seek help in interpreting results. This will ensure he builds a strong foundation of understanding across all areas of science.

(QCA 1999b, p. 53)

✎ Activity 7.7

Ask your induction tutor to provide you with some examples of reports on different pupils, including pastoral comments.
Discuss with him/her the following points:

- are there variations in departmental or individual teachers' practice?
- are there any ways that teacher comments could be improved?
- are targets for progress sufficiently clear and rigorous?
- in what ways could they involve the pupils when writing reports?
- how do the reports compare with your recollections of the reports you received from school?

It would be worth asking some pupils what *they* like/dislike about school reports.

References

Black, P. (1998) *Formative Assessment: Raising Standards Inside The Classroom*. London: School of Education, King's College.

Capel, S., Leask, M. and Turner, T. (1995) *Learning to Teach in the Secondary School*. London: Routledge.

Dearing, R. (1994) *The National Curriculum and its Assessment: Final Report.* London: SCAA.

Gipps, C. (1992) 'National Curriculum Assessment: a research agenda', *British Educational Research Journal* **18**(3), 277–86.

Gipps, C. (1994) *Beyond Testing: Towards a Theory of Educational Assessment.* London: Falmer Press.

Gipps, C. and Murphy, P. (1994) *A Fair Test? Assessment, Achievement and Equity.* Buckingham: Open University Press.

Gipps, C. and Stobart, G. (1993) *Assessment: A Teachers' Guide to the Issues.* London: Hodder & Stoughton.

Jones, J. (1994) *Assessment, Recording and Reporting Within The OFSTED Context.* Birmingham: Mill Wharf TCS course booklet.

Marshall, B. (1999) 'Exam obsession damages pupils', *Times Educational Supplement*, 3 September 1999, 15.

OFSTED (1995) *Guidance on the Inspection of Secondary Schools.* London: HMSO.

OFSTED (1996) *Subjects and Standards. Issues for school development arising from OFSTED inspection findings 1994–95.* London: HMSO.

Qualifications and Curriculum Authority (1999a) *Keeping Track.* London: QCA.

Qualifications and Curriculum Authority (1999b) *Assessment and Reporting Arrangements.* London: QCA.

Stobart, G., Elwood, J. and Quinlan, M. (1992) 'Gender Bias in Examinations: how equal are the opportunities?', *British Educational Research Journal* **18**(3), 261–76.

Chapter 8

Raising boys' achievement

Lads prefer larking to learning...Switching off and dropping out...Anti-school bias blights boys for life. These are just three typical headlines over recent press articles about the motivation and performance of boys in our schools, especially as far as GCSE results are concerned. A generation ago, the under-achievement of *girls* was identified as a national issue. Now, commentators are suggesting 'the future is female' and voicing worries over our 'lost boys' because *girls* are doing better than boys at every stage of school education. Ted Wragg has called it 'the gravest social problem we're facing'.

How to raise boys' achievement (while ensuring nothing that is done restrains *girls'* opportunities) is a topical issue engaging the attention of teachers and educationalists here and abroad. It is very relevant, therefore, to every newly qualified teacher. This section aims to consider:

1. The picture revealed by test and public examination results
2. Biological, social and economic factors
3. Factors linked to schooling and assessment
4. Strategies and good practice used in schools

The picture revealed by test and public exam results

The publication of schools' examination results has stimulated the current concerns about differences in gender performance. This is not the place to blind you with statistics. However, here are a few recent sets of figures that illustrate how boys are trailing behind girls, whatever the underlying causes:

- Figures from the 1998 pilot baseline assessments of children entering Year 1 reception classes revealed that girls consistently outstripped boys. Of the 6,732 children assessed, twice as many boys as girls fell into the bottom attainment category. Girls outnumbered boys by about 30 per cent in the top group. In number work, 35 per cent of girls reached the higher levels, compared with 29 per cent of boys. In reading and letter knowledge, a quarter reached the higher scores, compared with 16 per cent of boys.
- There is under-performance by boys in Key Stage 2 writing attainments. 1999 scores revealed almost two-thirds of girls achieved Level 4, compared with 45 per cent of boys. Reading is less of a problem: boys' scores shot up by 14 percentage points from 1998. Girls are only 6 per cent ahead, although the pattern varies from LEA to LEA. Boys have benefited from the concentration on guided reading in the literacy hour and the DfEE money for Year 6 booster classes, although another factor is that the 1999 tests were more 'boy-friendly' in terms of their content and presentation.
- At Key Stage 3, the three core subject reports sent to schools by the QCA show that girls continue to perform better than boys in English at the highest levels. In 1998

73 per cent achieved the national expectation of Level 5 or above, whereas only 57 per cent of boys did. Less worryingly, the reports reveal there are no overall differences in Mathematics and Science.

- Since 1987, the difference in the proportions of Year 11 girls and boys gaining 5-plus A*–C grades in England and Wales has steadily increased. The gap widened from 1.6 per cent in 1987 (the last year of O-levels) to 7.6 per cent in 1990 to 9.6 per cent in 1999. Also, only one in 30 entries by boys gained the coveted A*, compared with almost one in 20 by girls. However, it is not a case of the boys' performance worsening. Boys have actually improved their GCSE results in the 5-plus A*–C category, but not as rapidly as the girls.
- Even at Advanced Level, boys' traditional superiority is waning, with girls matching their proportion of A grades for the first time.

We should be wary of portraying 'boys' as a homogeneous group of under-achievers. Not all boys are 'victims' of the education system: research points to difficulties with particular groups, e.g. some white-working class or some Afro-Caribbean boys. Their worrying performance extends *beyond* tests and examinations to literacy, university admissions, special needs provision, truancy and crime. These press reports were collected in the space of just five days!

Boys in the news

Test results for 1997 show a similar gender gap to that in 1996, when 7-year-old boys were 9 per cent behind girls for reading and 10% for English, rising to a 15 per cent gap for 11-year-olds and 18 per cent at 14 (*Daily Telegraph*, 5 January 1998).

Last year, more girls achieved five good GCSE passes at grade C or above in every education authority in England, except Kensington and Chelsea (Wolverhampton *Express & Star*, 5 January 1998).

28,500 boys leave school each year with no qualifications, compared with 21,500 girls (*Guardian*, 5 January 1998).

Boys make up 83 per cent of pupils who are permanently excluded from school in England and Wales (*TES*, 9 January 1998).

Scotland Yard has warned that children aged between 14 and 16 are responsible for 40 per cent of London street crime. The majority are male, many of them illiterate (*Daily Telegraph*, 5 January 1998).

✎ Activity 8.1

Before reading any further, go through this short survey. Put ticks in the appropriate columns to indicate whether you think each one is true of the average boy or the average girl.

Once you have gone through the various aspects of this chapter, you should check to see if any of your views have changed.

Gender and Achievement – *What Do <u>You</u> Think?*

Which of these statements are true of the average girl and of the average boy?

	Girl	Boy
1 As a baby, speaks earlier		
2 Is spoken to more softly by parents		
3 Is more concerned with neat presentation		
4 Is noisier and more attention seeking		
5 Is more mature at the beginning of KS3		
6 Prefers short-term tasks		
7 Likes to have a good laugh		
8 Spends more time reading and chatting		
9 Spends more time doing homework		
10 Prefers doing, rather than talking		
11 Likes activities involving physical daring		
12 Less interested in characters/motives in stories		
13 Prefers sharing books with friends		
14 Likes non-fiction and technical books		
15 Spends less time playing computer games		
16 Likes to play more with mechanical toys		
17 Likes to be a clown or a 'toughie' in class		
18 Keen to be seen to do well		
19 Likes to prepare and revise in advance		
20 Thinks things will be 'alright on the night'		
21 Is more of a risk-taker		
22 Has a higher concentration span		
23 Is more committed to completing coursework		
24 Is better at reflective thinking		
25 Has more detailed plans for adult life		

Biological, social and economic factors

Researchers have identified various explanations for some boys under-achieving at school. They range from biological factors that begin in the womb and social influences on their early learning and performance, to the possibly superfluous role of males in a technological, service economy that readily employs females. And that's *before* we think about what happens in the classroom! Many explanations are speculative or stereotypical, while some of the issues touched on are complex.

Biological factors first. Research on the growing foetus has indicated that female ones can be observed moving their mouths at an earlier stage, which may reflect a pattern of advanced development from conception. Discoveries in scanning technology mean information on differences in brain function is greatly increasing our knowledge of gender thinking and behaviour. For example, research suggests that males and females differ in things like:

- spatial visualisation;
- sensitivity to sound and intonation, so girls learn language more quickly;
- how the brain processes thinking and language tasks, in that the relevant areas of the brain are more highly developed in females;

- sensitivity to the feelings of others, with females having an advantage as far as tact, social deftness and intuition are concerned.

However, there are dangers in having one's perceptions shaped by a sense of biological determinism, as seen in headlines like *Boys are oafish because they can't help it* or *The sensitive sex was born that way*. Much of the above research is still in its infancy, which makes it appropriate to distinguish between *evidence* for differences and *assertion* about their significance.

A more fruitful source of explanation lies in *social influences on boys' early learning and performance*. Differences reveal themselves in playgroups and then extend through the early years of primary school, as the following report shows.

Playgroup

Boys make straight for the construction toys or the bikes while the girls are playing in the home corner, doing a drawing or talking to an adult. Children have already developed clear ideas of what boys do and girls do. 'Boys are racing all around the garden being somebody else or being the leader. Girls – you find them sitting in a corner playing their quiet games,' were observations from playgroup staff...Each is practising different types of talk, a mother–child discussion as opposed to arresting a baddie, for instance.

Reception

Boys arrive with an interest in information books and...find reading schemes, based largely on stories about people, harder to get into. They may also be at a disadvantage in learning to write because they are less good with pencils...Even when boys and girls are following the same activity, like playing with Lego, they are doing it differently. Boys made vehicles or guns, using moveable parts, while girls made simple houses to use in a social game.

(MacLeod 1997, p. 3)

By age seven, boys and girls already have different attitudes to presentation, paying attention and socialising. Girls often play without supervision, and set their own rules and roles like adults. Boys, by contrast, are more noisy and attention seeking, liking to pretend they are cars or jet planes. No wonder girls start secondary school with greater maturity, work on-task and set high standards for themselves. You are likely to find that boys want to do things quickly, read less, do not take such care with presentation and like a laugh. They downplay their ability in case they appear to be 'boffins', 'nerds', 'swots' or 'keenos'.

This is *not* true for all boys, but the way some identify with Jack-the-lad macho values leads them to regard working hard as 'uncool'. Instead, you are likely to encounter what Ted Wragg calls 'the torpor of adolescence, when a deep grunt and a raised eyebrow are the most energetic responses you will ever get'! In that sense, we should be trying to change not just our approaches to pupil learning, but also the culture of masculinity that belittles learning.

Once in adolescence, many boys seem to prefer an experiential learning style. They have difficulty developing 'feminine' reflective traits, like analysis, discussion and expressing feelings. While you will see girls sitting and writing, boys will be opting for open discussions and physical involvement. They are more confident, self-assured and risk-taking. However, their attention span is a problem: the 'typical' 14-year-old boy concentrates for only 4–5 minutes, compared with 13 for girls.

There are profound issues, as well, to do with the *role of males in modern society*. Boys are losing male role models in their families as more families split. Since women tend to retain custody in such cases, it is likely that up to half today's children – here and in the USA – will grow up in a household without their natural father. Possibly linked to this is the increasing feminisation of primary school staff. So if boys in their formative years are finding themselves in homes and a world of learning not associated with men, they are not gaining exposure to the 'masculine' dimension of what growing up like a male is, or should be, like. Francis Fukuyama believes fathers can do certain things more easily than mothers, like moulding their sons' innate aggressiveness into positive channels.

Another possible factor is the uncertainty surrounding work prospects for boys, now that restructuring the economy has wiped out many traditional working class jobs. New employment markets are more akin to the flexibility and interpersonal skills of career-minded females. The psychological effect of their divorced fathers being relegated to the role of occasional playmates, or the increasing number of female 'breadwinners', *could* be instrumental in reducing motivation or self-respect in some boys at a crucial stage in their development. If so, it is likely to result in an antipathy to school as representing a system of hostile authority and meaningless work demands.

Factors linked to schooling and assessment

The 1993 OFSTED report, *Boys and English*, highlighted their poor literacy skills, narrower experiences of fiction and difficulty with affective aspects of English. Other surveys have noted a decline in boys' *reading* by the age of 14. Part of the problem is that boys have narrower preferences. They dislike poetry and most fiction (apart from sport, fantasy and action stories), preferring information books linked to their interests. Role models at home can have an effect. If the only people who encourage them to read are females in the family and their (largely female) primary teachers, getting absorbed in a book runs the risk of being branded a 'sissy', rather than masculine, pursuit.

There is a similar dichotomy in *writing*. Boys tend to express themselves in factual detail, while girls favour extended and reflective work. This means both sexes perform confidently on tasks they prefer, but whether these conform to teachers' and exam course expectations is another matter.

The introduction of *GCSE coursework*, requiring sustained attention and rewarding consistent effort, has reflected girls' more diligent approach via activities like portfolios, extended prose and research projects. By contrast, boys do not like to be seen to be diligent and committed to their work. Over-confidence is a common characteristic: they are inclined to be blasé about their prospects and then put their poor results down to having a 'bad day'. However, boys still perform well at A-level.

Assessments are only part of the problem. Boys' *perceptions of a subject*, the experiences they bring to it, and the type of demands a subject and its teachers make of them all exert an influence on performance. How far boys still rate subjects as stereotypically masculine or feminine has been the subject of various studies. Some boys may favour 'masculine' subjects as a way of reinforcing their identity. Their problem is that much of the work now done puts a premium on skills in which girls have an advantage. There is less emphasis on memorising and more on understanding. It points to an 'oestrogenisation' of the curriculum, including subjects like Maths, Physics, D&T and ICT for which boys have significant preferences.

✎ Activity 8.2
Look at the following two extracts from a GCSE English paper.
Which was written by a girl and which by a boy? How do they represent different interpretations of, and preferences for, writing?

Science vs poetry: two views of a demoiselle fly

Pupil A's response: The demoiselle fly in general has a short thorax, long abdomen and bulbous compound eyes. Type A has all these qualities, but differs from Type B in the following ways:
1. It has six long black legs with long hairs on top and lower parts of its legs. Type B only has four legs and has hairs on the bottom of its forelegs and top of its hindlegs only.
2. Type A has opaque wings which are short and wide. Type B has transparent wings which are notably longer and thinner than Type A's.
3. Type A has its abdomen segmented into fairly small parts, the end section tapering to a point. Type B's abdomen tapers downwards to make it triangular.

Pupil B's response: It is one of those lazy hot days in summer when everything is warm and very quiet. The trees surrounding the lake at the bottom of the hill are swaying silently and the ripples on the lake give the impression of peace and tranquility. At the end of the lake are reeds and lilies. Flies buzz dozily among the tall grasses. Bees laze among the pollen-filled lilies, drinking their sweet nectar, and the demoiselle flies perch motionless on the tall green fronds of the reeds. There are two in particular – one male, one female – that catch my eye as I lie against the sturdy trunk of an ancient oak. They are the most beautiful creatures I have ever seen, but they are both different...

(*Guardian Education*, 17 June 1997, p. 3).

Strategies and good practice used in schools

What you will want most as an NQT are some practical strategies to adopt for working effectively with boys. Fortunately, the issue is emerging from its infancy as far as research and publications are concerned. Much good work is taking place in schools, LEAs and universities. It is pleasing to note that our political masters have a positive view on the matter, too, judging by David Blunkett's recent call for teachers to turn boys on to reading by introducing them to action-packed tales like *Treasure Island, Frankenstein* or *The Time Machine*. Also, the new English curriculum requires specific provision to be made in the form of:

- offering 'non-literary' texts;
- making full use of boys' reading choices;
- more emphasis on concise analysis in writing (to complement imagination and expression);
- channelling boys' ability in spoken language into drama/role play.

More and more schools are committing themselves to strategies for improvement, although very few claim to have a blueprint for success. The starting points depend very much on the nature of the problem in each school and the systems already in place. Their various approaches include, in no particular order of importance:

- Use questionnaires to establish boys' attitudes to work and school.
- Mentor under-achievers, using sixth-formers or adults from business or industry.
- Use outside experiences, e.g. work placements, to give boys opportunities for success in a different context.
- One-to-one 'How's it going?' tutorials to encourage success, raise expectations and identify short-term personal targets in specific subject areas.

- Use of public praise for younger boys and more private praise for older ones.
- Give boys' efforts a positive profile in displays, awards or school marketing.
- Look closely at successful boys in the school. What makes for their success?
- Create a small working party of boys to offer advice on rewards for success.
- Encourage greater involvement in school musical or dramatic productions.
- Create a climate where academic pursuits are not seen as second best to sport, etc.
- Provide good role models of males who are achieving in various walks of life. Create a 'Where are they now?' photo display of recent leavers.
- Discuss gender issues overtly in assemblies and PSE periods.
- Single-sex teaching groups in core curriculum subjects.
- Use mixed seating arrangements to encourage boy–girl collaboration and sharing of learning styles.
- Monitor the gender balance in teaching sets to see if pupils are set by potential (real ability) rather than performance. Avoid demoting boys for bad behaviour.
- Analyse teachers' marking for any gender differentiation. Ensure work is marked for content rather than presentation. Encourage staff to make one comment of praise and give one hint for improvement.
- Give boys and girls the opportunity to experience different styles of learning, especially active learning, challenges, risk-taking, investigations and role-play.
- Structure lessons with quick-fire starts and longer tasks as the time progresses.
- Examine the involvement of boys and girls in question-and-answer sessions. Use specific questioning, e.g. 'Give three reasons . . .' or 'Find five points . . .'
- Monitor teachers' expectations of boys' and girls' behaviour and achievement.
- Target boys' reading and use resource materials that acknowledge boys' interests.
- Employ ways of enhancing narrative writing, e.g. writing frames, concept ladders.
- Greater use of computers and word processing across the curriculum.
- Explore gender stereotypes in the curriculum.
- Use of 'positive practice' posters, e.g. 'Please remember your homework diary', 'Quietly on the corridors – brains at work', 'This is a learning zone'.
- Raise parental awareness via an evening seminar and targeted newsletters.
- Secure parental support for boys via shared reading, homework support, use of positive encouragement and rewards, etc.
- Homework clubs and use of a variety of homework tasks.
- Cross-phase liaison and continuity to improve boys' reading and writing skills in Key Stages 2 and 3.
- Parenting classes for older secondary pupils, especially in areas where there is a preponderance of single-parent families and no male role model.

The reassuring news to communicate to NQTs is that there is a general purpose and direction to the ferment of research and activity taking place across the country. In other words, you are not on your own! The remainder of this section briefly surveys a couple of case studies of individual schools' activities.

Many of the changes in attitude which lead boys to start rejecting academic opportunities, in favour of messing around at the back of the classroom, are substantially rooted in:

- the educational challenges;
- the quality of teaching and learning; and
- the nature of pupil-teacher relationships found in any school.

Failure to address such issues can turn some boys away from learning, with the corollary of poor effort and behaviour, GCSE results that trail behind girls, and failure to secure training and employment. The last thing we need is an educational under-class of disfunctioning, disaffected boys for whom our lessons become, in the words of Carol Rumens, 'like a will read solemnly to the disinherited' (Bleach and Smith 1998).

CASE STUDY 1

Boys' motivation and performance in Key Stage 3

At Sneyd Community School, Walsall, staff used interviews to identify factors that lead some boys in Year 8 to 'go off the boil'. Their initial gust of enthusiasm for being in a new school may blow itself out, causing negative attitudes to set in. Although the potential under-achievers thought their educational experience was pleasant, staff uncovered several ingredients for disaffection that are probably found amongst boys in most secondary schools:

- *Teaching and learning*. *A diet of instruction and writing did not help motivation. They preferred role-play, investigations and use of IT.*
- *Reading and writing*. *There was a lack of interest in reading, except for magazines and soccer, war and horror books. They felt their work was judged excessively by its appearance.*
- *Homework*. *They questioned its value – work should be done on a 9–4 basis. They completed their work quickly and sometimes grudgingly.*
- *Attitudes to success*. *Effort improved if teachers recognised effort; if not, they didn't try hard. Also, being a 'keeno' harmed their credibility.*
- *Teacher–pupil relationships*. *Shouting and sarcasm inhibited effective learning. Warm and personable teachers helped them to progress.*

Following the interviews, staff held several meetings to discuss findings and air ideas. Out of these emerged key recommendations for trying to improve the quality of education enjoyed by the boys (and, by implication, the girls):

- *Using INSET and lesson observations to encourage staff to develop a repertoire of teaching styles to meet pupils' varied needs.*
- *Validating a variety of reading material and organising group reading and reviews, use of CD-ROMS, book weeks and visits by authors.*
- *Reviewing homework to include research, interviews, problem-solving and use of IT, thereby encouraging more independent learning.*
- *Creating a climate of achievement for all, e.g. rewarding groups of achievers and recognising effort of various kinds.*
- *Improving strategies for positive behaviour management to help teachers maintain a well-ordered but stimulating learning environment.*

These are five broad areas that seek to maintain boys' interest in learning and achievement. Some are practical steps; others involve a more fundamental shift in thinking. All are firmly rooted in good teaching and learning practice. Also, they are 'gender-inclusive'. Implementing them will do nothing to restrain girls' opportunities for continuing success.

(Bleach 1997, 14; 1998, 37–55)

CASE STUDY 2

Literacy is the crucial issue

These strategies have been piloted, implemented and reviewed by a number of schools in Kirklees LEA.

- Having avoided certain stock for its focus on male stereotypes and interests, has the English team now got books that boys want to read, will ask to read, will be excited to read? Is there a good range of available non-fiction? Contact your Library Support Services for ideas about the 'right kind' of stock to attract reluctant readers – who will be mainly boys.
- Choose books with good covers, showing boys as central characters.
- Occasionally make stories on tape available to pupils in order to keep alive their interest in good fiction.
- Encourage boys to pursue their reading related to specialist interests – computers, fishing and so on. Make it clear they might need to consult 'adult' texts on these subjects. Make sure that the School Library can cater for this through books, CD–ROMs and so on.
- Let some written responses to literary texts be non-empathic.
- Set up a series of visits of reader role models, with a balance of male and female. Try asking SMT, governors, parents, local councillors, sports-people, local celebrities and so forth.
- In each school newsletter, make sure that there is an item about reading.
- Encourage colleagues teaching in other areas of the curriculum to spend a little time unpicking the language used in their textbook. This should help to reinforce the message that reading is vital and that awareness of language use helps one to 'get the job done'.
- Use comic strip books and magazines in lessons – not all offer stereotyped or violent images.
- Some television series lead to 'spin off' books which may interest boys.
- Have displays encouraging boys to read. (Posters are available from the National Literacy Trust, 1A Grosvenor Gardens, London SW1W 0BD.)
- Present pupils with adult reading role models.
- Encourage boys who share enjoyment of a specific genre to set up a display with details of the genre, its authors and why it is popular.
- Use USSR (uninterrupted sustained reading in class) with attached, clearly focused activities.
- Offer structure in written tasks ('In your story, four things should happen to the central character. Discuss possibilities with your partner' or 'Each time you mention what a character does, also write what he/she feels.')

(Bradford 1996)

References

Bleach, K. (1997) 'Where did we go wrong?', *Times Educational Supplement*, 14 February 1997, 14.

Bleach, K. (1998) *Raising Boys' Achievement in Schools*. Stoke: Trentham Books.

Bleach, K. and Smith, J. (1998) 'Switching Off and Dropping Out?', *Topic* **20**(3) 1–5.

Bradford, W. (1996) *Raising Boys' Achievement*. Huddersfield: Kirklees LEA.

MacLeod, D. (1997) 'The gender divide', *Guardian Education*, 17 June 1997, 3.

OFSTED (1993) *Boys and English*. London: OFSTED.

Chapter 9
Pastoral issues

The vast majority of NQTs will start the first day as a paid, professional teacher with schemes of work prepared, textbooks and resources organised and set/class lists at the ready. This is understandable, given their enthusiasm for setting about teaching the knowledge, skills and understanding of their subject(s). However, we are all teachers of *children* as well, so pastoral roles and responsibilities should be regarded as equally important in the induction year, and beyond.

A teacher's wider professional duties will be varied and complex, so it is understandable that NQTs regard it as an area about which they feel some concern. This section deals with a selection of the most important aspects:

1. The pastoral goals of a school
2. The pastoral role of the form tutor
3. Dealing with parents
4. Child protection
5. Bullying.

The pastoral goals of a school

HMI (1989) has described the important role of pastoral care in the following terms:

The role of pastoral care
Pastoral care is concerned with promoting pupils' personal and social development and fostering positive attitudes through:

- the quality of teaching and learning
- the nature of relationships amongst pupils, teachers and adults other than teachers
- arrangements for monitoring pupils' overall progress – academic, personal and social – through specific pastoral structures and support systems
- extra-curricular activities and the school's ethos.

(HMI 1989)

A pastoral system operates most effectively, therefore, when it links together academic, personal and social dimensions of pupils' education in a systematic support structure. There should not be a pastoral–curricular dichotomy in teachers' roles. Rather, an interlinking pastoral approach contributes to the kind of overall school goals, relating to pupil support and guidance, cited by Lodge and Watkins (1996):

To offer support and guidance for pupil achievement by:

- providing a point of personal contact with every pupil and their parents in order to hear and understand their experience and their view of progress
- monitoring each individual pupil's progress and achievement across the whole curriculum and creating an overview of their approach to different learning tasks
- mobilising the resources of the wider educational, welfare, community and world of work networks to support and extend the experiences of all pupils.

(Lodge and Watkins 1996, p. 2)

Responsibility for the first goal obviously rests with the form tutor and the outcomes inform progress towards the second goal. Given the subject-based nature of the secondary curriculum, it is important to build a cross-departmental picture of each pupil's performance. The third goal recognises that pupils' development is enhanced by links to the range of local support agencies outside school that have further skills, experiences and resources to offer.

Haydon and Lambert (1992) classify the many tasks identified with pastoral care, which require a coordinated approach in various settings, e.g. subject teaching, tutorial meetings, careers, personal and social education:

- *pastoral casework* – any aspect of a pupil's progress, achievement and development, involving his learning or helping resolve problems like bullying;
- *pastoral curriculum* – the personal/social skills and knowledge pupils need at school and outside life, which schools pursue in subject lessons and a PSE programme of study;
- *pastoral management* – the planning, monitoring, reviewing and communication between teams and individuals that underpin support for pupils' academic progress, personal development, behaviour and attendance.

In most schools, all these strands are brought together in a written policy, which includes how pastoral provision will be monitored and reviewed, and how it links with overall school aims and with other policies of the school.

The pastoral role of the form tutor

The form tutor in the secondary school has defined pastoral responsibilities towards a particular group of pupils. Vlaeminke (1995) believes that developing a sound relationship with your tutor group, based on mutual trust and respect, should prove to be a very satisfying part of the induction year. You will prove to be the lynchpin who knows pupils better than anyone else.

Being a form tutor will occupy a couple of hours each week when you are in direct contact and relationship with your form, not to mention informal staffroom consultations and large quantities of paperwork. Your school should ensure you are prepared for the various aspects of this role, including the legal and contractual elements. To give just three examples, you need:

- guidance in the mechanics of register marking so that absences of various kinds are accurately recorded;
- a scheme of work and resource materials for the school's PSE programme;
- advice and support in dealing with the girl who sobs continuously because her father

has just left home; the boy with cuts and bruises on his neck and shoulders; the sharp letter of complaint from parents objecting to the absence of set homework in Maths for the last half term!

In other words, you will need ongoing training and support for the variety of everyday situations and challenges that most tutors face – and which often have to be sorted in a short registration period, at break, lunchtime or one of your precious non-contact periods.

To help get it right, you should be provided with a *tutorial role description*. While it will not list all the tasks that need to be carried out, a carefully worded role description will help you to develop a clear picture in your mind of its main aspects. The Case Study printed after Activity 9.1 is a typical summary of what a secondary school expects.

Nathan (1995) offers a useful summary of the *important aspects of the tutorial role* that apply to teachers:

- routine tasks have to be carried out, many of which are humdrum and time-consuming, but they keep the school going;
- the tutor is central to the administrative and documentary procedures relating to pupils;
- a tutor's organisational effectiveness, good timekeeping, attention to school uniform and care of the classroom will help maintain a high standard of conduct by the pupils;
- it is necessary to balance the two roles of subject teacher and tutor so that neither is concentrated on at the expense of the other;
- the right kind of relationship must be developed with pupils, because they are very quick to pick up and, if it suits them, adopt teachers' attitudes.

The responsibility that you must exercise for the pastoral care of your form is likely to present various issues and problems that need resolving. The demands they make on you will differ from school to school. Some tutors will find they have a relatively easy passage during induction, while others might face a whole cluster of problems. The following Activity explores a number of common situations.

✎ Activity 9.1

Discuss the following situations with either your induction tutor or a head of year. How would you try to deal with each one, putting emphasis on the support you might wish to seek from more experienced staff?

- A parent sends a letter asking you to talk to her daughter to find out why she is miserable and uncooperative at home.
- A member of your tutor group tells you he has stolen money from home.
- A pupil asks if he can talk to you in confidence. He says he won't tell you anything until you can give him that assurance.
- You half-hear a furtive conversation about drugs in one corner of the classroom.
- One of your form is repeatedly late for registration in the morning. You speak to her about it, but there is no improvement.
- At the end of the day, a pupil runs back into school crying. Some older pupils have picked on him.
- You notice that a girl in your tutor group smells badly of body odour and her hair and clothes are dirty.
- One of the girls in your form says she thinks she is pregnant. She is reluctant to go to the doctor or have a pregnancy test.

(Vlaeminke 1995, p. 53)

CASE STUDY

Role of the Form Tutor

Overall responsibility

The Form Tutor is responsible for the day-to-day pastoral welfare and oversight of his/her pupils. The Form Tutor should spend time getting to know pupils to the point that he/she becomes the major source of information in terms of their background, interests, school records, feelings towards school, etc. The Form Tutor, therefore, should actively promote the academic, pastoral and social well-being of the pupils and monitor the effect of school policies on them.

Line responsibility

- Responsible to the appropriate Head of Year.
- Responsible for pupils in his/her form.
- Responsible for liaison with all other staff, Special Needs staff as appropriate, and parents.

Main responsibilities

- To establish an understanding and knowledge of pupils in his/her care.
- To monitor the welfare of each child.
- To monitor the academic and personal performance of each child.
- As a result of the above three points, to offer guidance and suggest/take appropriate courses of action.
- To establish standards of behaviour, dress and courtesy with the tutor group in accordance with school policy.
- To deliver the Social Education programme.
- To make pupils aware of, and implement, aspects of school policy as and when they arise.

Administration

- To update all pastoral and academic files as necessary.
- To monitor and encourage the attendance/punctuality of each child.
- To complete whole-school administrative tasks as and when requested.
- To maintain an accurate register as outlined in the school policy.

(Sneyd Community School, Walsall)

Dealing with parents

New teachers are often apprehensive about joining the staff, getting to grips with pupils, coping with paperwork and meeting parents, especially at a parents' evening! They have had only a short time in which to learn all the pupils' names, and now they are being called on to speak with authority about their progress, ability, social development, future SATs levels or GCSE grades.

Contact with parents is an essential and unavoidable part of any school's public relations. Inevitably, your lack of experience and status might send a shudder down your spine, but don't forget that many parents are equally daunted by meeting teachers! So you will need guidance about how to handle occasions like:

- parents' consultation evenings;
- letters and telephone calls that express grievances;
- dealing with angry or upset parents making unexpected individual visits;
- parent helpers in the classroom or on visits.

Parents' evenings – Official feedback sessions to enable parents to discuss and raise issues about their child's progress vary in format, depending on the school. However, the following general points should help you handle your first parents' evening successfully.

- Outline your comments in advance and take assessment records, exercise books and school reports to the meeting. Parents are easier to convince when faced with evidence. Obviously, you must be able to put faces to names!
- Check seating arrangements to make sure you are next to a more experienced colleague who can step in if an exchange becomes heated.
- Find out if there are any parents who have reputations for being awkward or argumentative, so that a colleague can lend you support if it is needed.
- You need to personify for parents the professional image of a teacher, so dress formally and stand up to greet them when they arrive.
- Many parents are naturally defensive about their children, so it is worth treading warily until you are sure of your ground. At the same time, they also appreciate being given a full and honest picture.
- Be constructive and analytical, even if it's difficult to say many positive things. It shows you are being professional, rather than personal, in your comments. Offer ways forward and targets for action on issues like punctuality, homework, etc.
- Avoid a 'them and us' situation by using 'we'. This shows that you wish to work together with parents.
- If parents will not accept what is said, politely stand your ground and give chapter and verse about incidents. Bring in a second opinion if necessary.
- There is usually little privacy at parents' evenings, so don't let argumentative or unpleasant exchanges develop.
- If a parent has an axe to grind about an issue, try to bring the conversation back to the topic in hand. If this does not work, politely refer them to the relevant colleague.
- Keep to schedule with your appointments. If they find themselves in long queues, parents are inclined to become irritable.
- When the interview has gone as far as it can, sum up by restating what each of you will do for the child and what you hope to achieve.

Letters and phone calls – Unless they are purely routine, do not respond to them on your own. A sensible move is to refer the letter or call to the head of year and get advice, especially if the communication is critical or unfair.

Angry parents – At some time or another, every teacher has a close encounter of the troublesome kind with a parent. This can happen at a consultation evening or on an unscheduled visit. Their behaviour often arises from worries about their child; on other occasions, it is the product of misunderstanding, awkwardness or downright truculence! Initially, you should be courteous but firm, and inform a senior colleague right away if confronted unexpectedly. During a difficult discussion, you should give a considered answer, rather than making a knee-jerk comment. While putting across a definite point of view, avoid belittling parents or putting them in a corner.

Parents as helpers – Parents are sometimes invited into classrooms to work with children and teachers, although this is more the case in primary schools. Nathan (1995) offers the following tips on making the best use of parents:

- become familiar with the school's practice on using parent-helpers;
- ask colleagues how they use parents;
- make the parent-helpers welcome in the classroom;
- discuss learning outcomes with them so they can see what is happening in the classroom;
- organise specific activities for the helpers;
- ask parents what tasks *they* enjoy doing;
- always remember to thank parents for their help at the end.

The great majority of parents actually want their children to do well at school. They appreciate advice regarding how to help them do that. They also want them to behave well and have a right to be informed if they do not. The fact is that both teachers and parents share the same goal of wanting to bring out the best in children, so draw encouragement from that.

Child protection

Through their daily contact with pupils, teachers are in key position to identify children suffering abuse and try to help them. Although only newly qualified, you might be the first person on the staff who had an inkling that something was amiss. Perhaps you are the only person in whom the child is prepared to confide. So it is crucial that you are aware of your school's child protection procedures.

The means by which abuse will be prevented may be summarised as follows:

A caring school ethos	which promotes the self-esteem of the individual and has a child-centred philosophy
Clear policies	for sex education, health education, equal opportunities, behaviour and bullying
A curriculum	which permits pupils to solve problems, form judgements, make decisions and choices; which offers opportunities to discuss emotions, relationships, good and bad secrets, safe and unsafe touches, bullying, assertiveness and parenting skills
Classroom management	which encourages independence, self-confidence and assertiveness
Good links	with parents or carers, and other professionals working with children
Respect for the child	as far as his/her colour, gender, race or creed are concerned

The 1989 *Children Act* places duties on various agencies, including schools, to assist local authority social services acting on behalf of children in need or enquiring into allegations of abuse. Adults working with children must be able to recognise suspected child abuse and know what action to take. The teacher's role is to 'act on suspicion' by referring or reporting observations. The investigative role belongs to the police or social services. Schools are legally obliged to appoint a 'named' senior member of staff to whom all cases of suspected abuse must be reported. That person then makes referrals as appropriate, maintains an 'at risk' register, consults with outside agencies, liaises with a 'named' Governor and is generally responsible for child protection procedures in the school.

The children's rights and needs fall into the following categories, each of which the great majority of parents recognise consciously or unconsciously.

Children's needs
- The need for physical care and protection from preventable harm.
- The need for bodily growth and exercise of physical and mental function.
- The need for love and security and the opportunity to relate to others.
- The need for new experiences and help in relating to the environment by way of organising and mastering age-appropriate levels of responsibility.
- The need for intellectual development.

(Walsall Area Child Protection Committee Procedures)

Defining child abuse is difficult, in that different people in different branches of the 'caring professions' have their own definitions. However, here is one working definition:

Defining abuse
A child is considered to be abused or at risk by parents/carers when the basic needs of the child are not being met through avoidable acts of either commission or omission. Four categories of abuse are commonly used to classify abusive behaviour: *physical injury, emotional abuse, neglect* and *sexual abuse*.

(Walsall Area Child Protection Committee Procedures)

Abuse happens to children of both sexes, all ages and all backgrounds. It may be hard to detect and will usually need both social and medical assessment. As a rough guide, the following may be indicators that something is amiss:

- changes in behaviour or reactions;
- overheard remarks which arouse suspicion;
- bruises or scratches not normally associated with accidental injury;
- burns or scalds;
- symptoms of neglect;
- behaviour with sexual overtones inappropriate to the child's age or development;
- a sudden drop in school performance;
- a sudden or marked reluctance to participate in PE.

A school's child protection policy will contain more information about accidental and non-accidental injury, together with more detailed signs. In themselves, they do not prove abuse, but they may *suggest* it, particularly if a child repeatedly exhibits such signs. To avoid the equal risks of either ignoring signs or jumping to unwarranted conclusions, you must *always consult your school's 'named' senior colleague.*

Bullying

No school in the country can truthfully say that no bullying takes place on its premises. Unfortunately, it seems to be part of human nature for some individuals to intimidate less forceful people to some degree. That makes bullying a difficult and sensitive issue to address, yet it must be done because it is a major concern to pupils, parents, staff and the public at large.

Bullying can be physical, verbal or emotional, and committed by a single person or a group. Incidents can include:

- name-calling
- teasing
- malicious gossip
- intimidation
- damaging/stealing property
- extortion
- violence and assault
- ostracising
- punching/kicking/jostling
- damaging school work.

Reasons for being a victim may be based on race, gender or class; newness in the school; a crisis in the child's family; or disability or difference of any kind. Victims are more likely to be children who are not assertive, loners with few friends, anxious children, younger children, and those outside a social group. *Reasons for being a bully* may arise from having been the victim of intimidation at some time; enjoyment of power or creating fear; copying behaviour seen at home or on television. Boys often bully younger children of both sexes; girls often use verbal abuse and ostracism from the peer group against other girls. Onlookers who condone bullying become accomplices.

A victim may demonstrate some of all of the following *signs of bullying* (which might also be indicative of child abuse):

- becoming withdrawn
- erratic attendance
- deterioration of work
- general unhappiness
- spurious illness
- late arrivals
- isolation
- bed wetting and other signs
- desire to remain with adults
- personality change.

Your schools will have an *anti-bullying strategy* with which you must become familiar in terms of knowing how to report incidents, take firm action and encourage children to work against intimidation via PSE or other programmes. General points of good practice for you to observe include:

- stressing to pupils that to watch an incident is to condone it;
- be aware of, and stop, any racist or sexist language;
- stress the need for, and reward, non-aggressive behaviour;
- stress to parents the unacceptability of bullying and 'hitting back';
- support the victim's need for self-esteem and self-value;
- find out *why* the bully is bullying.

✎ Activity 9.2

Ask your induction tutor to arrange for you to be attached to a teacher with a pastoral responsibility, during the first hour of morning school.
You could undertake one or more of the following activities:

- log the variety of activities, pupil interviews, telephone calls, etc. that take place
- compile a brief case study of a particular incident with a pupil
- discuss with the teacher what he/she feels are the positive and negative aspects of the job
- sit in on a meeting with a parent
- compile a list of the outside services with which he/she collaborates.

References

Haydon, G. and Lambert, D. (1992) *Professional Studies: Tutor Support Pack*. London: University of London Institute of Education.

HMI (1989) *Pastoral Care in Secondary Schools*. London: DES.

Lodge, C. and Watkins, C. (1996) 'Pastoral Care', *Managing Schools Today*, March 1996.

Nathan, M. (1995) *The New Teacher's Survival Guide*. London: Kogan Page.

Vlaeminke, M. (1995) *The Active Mentoring Programme 2: Developing Key Professional Competences*. Cambridge: Pearson Publishing.

Chapter 10

Special educational needs

Kevan Bleach and Rod Blaine

The Standards for the Award of QTS and the Induction Standards emphasise that newly qualified teachers should be familiar with the Code of Practice on the identification and assessment of pupils with special educational needs (SEN). So gaining an understanding of the challenges and opportunities presented by their wide-ranging needs is a key part of every NQT's induction.

This chapter seeks to contribute to that understanding by examining:

1. The statutory framework for SEN
2. Definitions of SEN
3. Stages of SEN assessment
4. Putting SEN policy into practice
5. The qualities of a teacher of SEN children.

The statutory framework for SEN

Children's basic right to share in the whole curriculum is enshrined in the 1988 Education Act. For many schools, this requirement to provide full entitlement and access confirmed their existing commitment to make provision for the needs of individual pupils with any kind of learning difficulty. Indeed, the term 'special needs' had been introduced in the Warnock Report (1978) and the subsequent 1981 Act.

The statutory framework for SEN was extended in the 1993 Education Act by:

- stating the definition of 'special educational needs';
- reaffirming a commitment to mainstream education for SEN pupils *unless*: (i) it is incompatible with parents' wishes, (ii) their learning difficulties require provision only available at a special school or (iii) the placement is not compatible with the efficient education of other pupils or the efficient use of resources;
- introducing a Code of Practice for Special Needs for LEAs and schools;
- setting time limits on statutory assessments and statements;
- assessing and monitoring each child (whether statemented or not) according to a staged process;
- extending parental roles and choices;
- establishing independent SEN tribunals;
- enhancing the role of the Special Educational Needs Coordinator (SENCO), who oversees provision on a whole-school basis.

In particular, the *Code of Practice on the Identification and Assessment of SEN* (DFE 1994) builds on Warnock and subsequent legislation. It provides for the assessment and statementing of pupils with SEN within a clearly defined five-stage model, with increased parental rights in terms of involvement, choice of school and right of appeal. Schools have access to educational psychologists, educational welfare officers and other support agencies.

Principles of the Code of Practice
- Special educational needs must be addressed.
- Recognition of a continuum of needs and provision.
- Greatest possible access to a broad and balanced curriculum.
- Most children with SEN will be in mainstream, with no statement; many children with statements will be in mainstream.
- Action in the early years: LEA and the health and social services.
- Partnership between parents and their children, schools, LEAs and other agencies.

National Children's Bureau

The Code of Practice involves a statutory duty for the governors of every school to make provision for SEN pupils. Part of this duty is to produce a school policy involving all staff. Every teacher, including NQTs, must also be aware of the school's procedures for identifying, assessing and making provision. The aspects of the Code that outline the role of the subject teacher and the form tutor are of particular relevance so that you have guidance on what to do if you have concerns about an individual child. As part of its inspection procedures, OFSTED scrutinises the effectiveness of these practices.

Definitions of SEN

There are various approaches to defining 'special educational needs'. What they share in common is that the term 'special' implies something out of the ordinary in a world where needs are individual and diverse. It has been estimated that about one in five pupils will require special needs to be met at some point during their school career. The Code itself defines SEN as 'a child [who] has a learning difficulty which calls for special educational provision to be made for him or her'. The term 'learning difficulty' refers to a child who has:

- a significantly greater difficulty in learning than the majority of children of the same age;
- a disability which either prevents or hinders the child from making use of the educational facilities of a kind provided for children of the same age in schools within the area of the LEA.

The National Curriculum Council grouped SEN pupils under four main headings:

Categories of SEN pupil
1. Pupils with exceptionally severe learning difficulties including those with profound and multiple learning difficulties...or exceptionally severe learning difficulties resulting from, for example, multi-sensory impairment.
2. Pupils with other learning difficulties including those with mild, moderate or specific learning difficulties, or those with emotional and behavioural difficulties.
3. Pupils with physical or sensory impairment.
4. Exceptionally able pupils.

(NCC 1993)

One of the main assumptions underpinning SEN provision is that, wherever possible, it should be in mainstream schools. The inclusion of SEN pupils has had a considerable impact on the deployment of staff and pupils' daily routines. Schools are expected to provide differentiated materials so that all children can be taught in mainstream lessons. SEN teachers may support individual pupils in class, give advice on suitable teaching methods and resources or, at times, they may withdraw pupils for additional help with literacy and numeracy. An important part of your job will be to liaise and work closely with support teachers and classroom assistants in preparing lessons and resources in advance.

Capel *et al.* (1995) stress it is likely that a proportion of the pupils taught by any NQT will fall into the second category identified in the above quotation. Some needs might be temporary, in that a child may be emotionally upset because of a home situation that is later remedied, or they might be suffering from long-term problems, such as dyslexia or other specific learning difficulties. The third group includes pupils who have hearing, visual or physical disabilities. Their needs create a variety of challenges for teachers which are met by curricular, resource or even site adaptation (e.g. wheelchair access to labs).

✎ Activity 10.1

Compile a brief report about one SEN pupil that you teach. Concentrate on the pupil's weaknesses *and* strengths, describing adaptations to classroom work that are made to take account of his/her special needs, and outlining the use made of the support teacher or classroom assistant (if appropriate).

Stages of SEN assessment

The following are the five stages of SEN identification and assessment set out in the Code of Practice. Stages 1 and 2 are school-based, involving a continuous process of planning, intervention and review. Stage 3 entails the use of external support agencies, such as hearing or vision-impaired services. Stage 4 is the statutory period of assessment by the LEA – schools, external agencies or parents may refer pupils. Stage 5 is when the statementing of special educational needs takes place.

The stages should not be seen as hurdles over which a pupil has to jump. They are more a placement for a particular level of need. There are proposals that a new Code of Practice will be introduced, with a new name to avoid the problem of stages being perceived as hurdles. Stage 1 is likely to be removed, Stage 2 may be called 'Support' and Stage 3 'Support Plus'.

The *Individual Education Plan* (IEP) is a teacher-produced document setting out individual pupil's specific learning difficulties and needs, and how they will be met. It has a vital part to play in schools' strategic planning, although for some schools the number that need to be produced and reviewed constitutes a significant responsibility. Capel *et al.* (1997) state that the *Individual Education Plan* (IEP) should set out:

- the nature of the pupil's learning difficulty;
- SEN provision;
- staff involved, including external agencies where appropriate;
- frequency of support, specific programmes and activities;
- materials and equipment;
- help from parents/carers at home;
- targets to be achieved in a given time;
- any pastoral care or medical requirements;
- monitoring and assessment arrangements;
- a review date.

Stage	Personnel	Action
Stage 1	Class/subject teacher. Consultation with SENCO.	Identification of needs. Awareness of needs by subject teachers. Gather information. Liaise with parents. Monitor and review child's progress. Differentiation within mainstream lessons. Inform head teacher.
Stage 2	SENCO.	Identification of needs. Provision of Individual Education Plan (IEP). Regular monitoring and reviews, usually termly. Continue liaison with parents and head teacher.
Stage 3	SENCO and external support agencies.	As for Stage 2, but also involve external support agencies. Consult with head teacher on referral to LEA for consideration re statutory review. Annual reviews.
Stage 4	Local Education Authority.	Consider need for statutory assessment and make multi-disciplinary assessment by all agencies if necessary.
Stage 5	Local Education Authority.	Consider need for statement of SEN and, if appropriate, make statement. Provision by LEA. IEP. Annual review.

It is important that you understand information in the IEP will be available to you as a subject teacher. In turn, you are expected to give regular feedback on pupils' progress, which is why it is important to keep accurate records. As a form tutor, you may be asked to attend formal review meetings with pupils, parents and other professionals. In the most recent HMI survey (1999) on the SEN Code of Practice, it was reported that some schools make effective use of IEPs in setting challenging learning targets and reviewing their pupils' progress – but many do not. It was found that pupils' views are rarely sought when preparing or reviewing IEPs and that greater linkage needs to be made with school literacy policies.

For the significant majority of SEN children, no statutory assessment will be necessary. However, where the LEA makes a *statement of special educational needs*, following assessment, it will contain:

- factual details about the child;
- what the statutory assessment reveals about the pupil's special needs;
- what the LEA maintains is needed to meet the pupil's needs;
- details of the school in which provision will be made;
- what the external agencies report about the pupil's non-educational needs;
- how those non-educational needs will be met.

As stated earlier, schools are required to have an identified *Special Educational Needs Coordinator* (SENCO). In a small school, the head or deputy may take on the role. The key responsibilities of the post-holder include:

- day-to-day operation of the school's SEN policy;
- advising class and subject teachers about the needs of their pupils;
- taking the lead in managing provision for pupils at stages 2 to 5;
- updating and overseeing the records for all SEN pupils on the register;
- working with parents of SEN pupils;
- liaising with external agencies.

✎ Activity 10.2

Look carefully at the Individual Education Plan of an SEN pupil taught by you. To what extent do you need to adjust your lesson preparation to ensure the identified needs of that pupil are met? It would be informative to share your views with your SENCO or one of his/her support staff.

Putting SEN policy into practice

Every school must have an SEN policy statement identifying how pupils with learning difficulties and disabilities can have access to the curriculum. It is vital that you acquaint yourself with the document produced by your new school. You should find it refers to:

- arrangements in the school for children with special needs;
- any specialist provision offered by the school (e.g. hearing-impaired unit);
- admission arrangements for SEN pupils;
- the school's objectives for SEN pupils;
- how resources for them are allocated;
- procedures for screening, record keeping, monitoring and reviewing;
- name and roles of the SENCO and other staff responsible for SEN pupils;
- teaching strategies and the use of support services;
- plans for appropriate in-service training;
- use of facilities outside the school (e.g. links with special schools);
- how social services and other agencies carry out their responsibilities;
- how children are protected from harm and abuse;
- any arrangements for medical treatment;
- how parents are involved in discussions about their children;
- how governors make sure pupils receive their SEN provision;
- how staff are kept informed about pupils with special needs;
- ways in which such pupils take part in the life and work of the school.

OFSTED inspections scrutinise how far a school's policy (on *any* topic) reflects a satisfactory whole-school approach and actually puts it into practice. The extract in the following Case Study shows how an SEN policy can be framed to try to ensure that what actually happens in a school reflects the Code of Practice.

CASE STUDY

Extracts from an SEN policy statement

Philosophy	Principles	Procedures	Performance
2. All pupils should have equal access to the school building.	2.1 The building made accessible to pupils of all disabilities as far as resources allow.	2.1.1 Consult with outside agencies to make adjustments to access/facilities. 2.1.2 Consultation with the LEA to provide facilities. 2.1.3 Termly meetings of SENCO and Site Director.	SENCO and Site Director monitor provision.
3. All pupils should leave school with some form of certification.	3.1 Pupils follow GCSE, vocational or other external courses in Y10–11.	3.1.1 SENCO meets with Head of Y9 and Form Tutors at beginning of KS4 subject choice process.	SENCO to liaise with Head of Examinations and Heads of Department, and report to Governors.
	3.2 All pupils leave school with an ROA document.	3.2.1 Form Tutors ensure SEN pupils have extra time and facilities to produce final ROA statements.	Head of Y11 to monitor and report to SENCO.
	3.3 All pupils have opportunity to become COMPACT graduates.	3.3.1 Clear targets are set and SEN pupils are closely and frequently monitored regarding progress.	Head of Y11 to monitor and report to SENCO.
6. There should be close cooperation between parents and school.	6.1 Parents will be kept informed of their child's progress.	6.1.1 All parents of register pupils receive letter explaining purpose. 6.1.2 Those on Stage 2+ receive IEP information. 6.1.3 Parents receive information about review procedures and dates. 6.1.4 SEN Y7 Parents' Evening held in September. 6.1.5 Dissatisfied parents urged to contact SENCO/Head/Chair of Governors.	SENCO regularly reports to Governors.
7. All teachers are responsible for SEN pupils in their classes.	7.1 Teachers provide differentiated work for register pupils.	7.1.1 Schemes of work specify differentiation. 7.1.2 Subject and SEN staff consult on lessons. 7.1.3 A fixed percentage of capitation to be spent on SEN resources. 7.1.4 Enhanced staffing for withdrawal and support.	Department SEN representative to monitor schemes. School SMT monitors curriculum. SENCO reports to Governors.
	7.2 INSET provided for all staff.	7.2.1 SENCO represented on INSET committee. 7.2.2 SENCO updates SMT on all SEN developments. 7.2.3 SENCO issues SEN bulletin to all departments.	INSET coordinator monitors availability of courses. Minutes of SMT meetings. File of bulletins.

(Sneyd Community School: Walsall)

The qualities of a teacher of SEN children

Finally, it is worth reflecting on what makes a good teacher of SEN pupils. Phinn (1997) suggests ten key qualities that deserve cultivation.

Understanding	• Makes an effort to understand how some pupils struggle with schoolwork. • Tailors work to their needs. • Does not repeatedly respond to their efforts in negative ways.
Encouragement	• Offers opportunities for all pupils to speak. • Encourages them to find more exact ways of saying things. • Shows interest in what they say. • Realises pupils like to have their efforts recognised.
Sensitivity	• Knows all pupils need to feel success. • Builds on what pupils already know and can do by advising, encouraging, intervening and challenging. • Guides each pupil to individual achievement and success.
Expectation	• Encourages pupils to concentrate. • Provides challenging work and has high expectations. • Realises pupils have insights into human nature. • Enables them to talk and write with humour, directness and imagination.
Respect	• Believes all pupils matter, however difficult or disruptive. • Realises understanding and respect from a trusted adult will tap their interests and values.
Challenge	• Provides balanced, appropriate and challenging activities through differentiated tasks. • Encourages pupils to discuss and read for themselves.
Creativity	• Is open-minded, optimistic and creative. • Captures pupils' imagination and appeals to their sense of humour. • Makes work relevant to their own experiences.
Planning and organisation	• Produces clear schemes of work and practical documentation on statemented pupils. • Regularly monitors own practice and reviews pupils' progress and attainment.
Effective classroom management	• Has a purposeful and well-ordered working environment. • Aims to develop choice and independent working by pupils. • Adjusts to pupils' changing needs and moods. • Deals with misbehaviour calmly.
A sense of humour	• Has a well-developed sense of humour. • Experiences a sense of shared enjoyment with pupils.

(Abridged from Phinn 1997, p. 26)

References

Capel, S., Leask, M. and Turner, T. (1995) *Learning to Teach in the Secondary School.* London: Routledge.

Capel, S., Leask, M. and Turner, T. (1997) *Starting to Teach in the Secondary School.* London: Routledge.

DFE (1994) *Code of Practice on the Identification and Assessment of Special Educational Needs.* London: DFE.

DES (1978) *Special Education Needs* (The Warnock Report). London: HMSO.

HMI (1999) *The SEN Code of Practice: Three Years On (IEPs).* London: OFSTED.

National Curriculum Council (1993) *Special Needs and the National Curriculum.* York: NCC.

Phinn, G. (1997) 'Just how special are you?', *Times Educational Supplement*, 10 January 1997, 26.

Chapter 11

Meeting the challenge of the able child

A small minority of teachers may express an ethical reservation about doing anything that could be construed as fostering 'elitism' within the comprehensive system. However, it is important to recognise that each child has *equal value* and *individual needs*. It does not mean everybody has to be the same! Another mistake is to suppose that able pupils will fully develop their talents in any circumstances. In fact, they need as much teaching and guidance as other pupils. Accordingly, those with marked academic advantages deserve assistance, and must be encouraged and supported to make the best educational achievement within the context of the non-selective, maintained sector.

A number of influences have caused increasing recognition of the need to provide for the most able within our primary and secondary schools:

- HMI and OFSTED note that the quality of teaching and learning for *all* pupils is enhanced in schools that meet the needs of the able;
- the DfEE recommends arrangements for able pupils should be included in every school's prospectus;
- there is a growing interest in differentiation in order to provide appropriate levels of work for pupils across the ability range;
- more and more schools are applying for specialist status in terms of technology, foreign languages or the arts;
- the National Curriculum provides for able pupils by the 'exceptional performance' classification and extension SATs, while GCSE offers the A* grade;
- schools operate in a competitive market environment, so it is important in prospective parents' eyes to maximise each child's potential;
- the global economy, technological innovations and unemployment mean we must nurture invention and innovation in our able children;
- our international competitors – particularly the Pacific Rim countries – have policies to provide for bright children.

This chapter looks at ways newly qualified teachers can contribute to a school's implementation of provision for its talented children. The following aspects are explored:

1. Defining the 'able' pupil
2. Identifying and recognising able pupils
3. Curriculum provision
4. Organisational strategies
5. Teaching methodology.

Defining the 'able' pupil

There is no exact definition of an 'able' pupil. Nevertheless, for practical purposes the following two attempts at definition give a general view.

Who are the more able?

To be regarded as more able is to be outstanding in general or specific abilities in a relatively broad or narrow field.

(Ogilvie 1973)

Those for whom the curriculum followed by the majority of their peers does not always provide sufficient challenge and opportunity for development.

(Tilsley 1992)

Human intelligence is a complex affair: there are various identifiable areas in which pupils may be very able. The work of Eric Ogilvie (1973) and the US Office of Education in the early 1970s suggested the following categories, later echoed by Howard Gardner's view (1983, 1991) that there are seven types of intelligence:

- general intelligence
- creative thinking ability
- general academic ability
- specific subject ability
- artistic and creative talent
- mechanical ingenuity
- psychomotor and performing skills
- leadership qualities
- processing ideas and information.

If high ability extends beyond purely intellectual talents, teaching methods that work through, and aim at, all these talents should be used. Only a small minority of pupils are broadly gifted, academic 'all-rounders' who do well at almost everything they undertake. A much larger proportion excels in one or a few areas, such as Art, Maths, sport or the performing arts. Eyre (1995) offers another perspective on the issue. According to the SEN Code of Practice, about two per cent of pupils have severe learning problems. However, a further 18 per cent may have either a specific learning difficulty or problems at some time in their school life. Thus, it is reasonable to expect a similar distribution at the top of the ability scale. That is why it is important to maintain a fluid definition of ability, so that it becomes *inclusive*, rather than exclusive. Our ambition should be to widen the pool of ability, not to restrict it. One Devon school told the *Times Educational Supplement* (29 September 1995) that its approach is to provide challenging work for all pupils, and then step back to see if they respond.

Identifying and recognising able pupils

It is vital for you to know which pupils have high ability – and the nature of that ability – if provision is to be made. Otherwise, recognition is not made or occurs later. Dickinson

(1982) relates the anecdote about one of David Bellamy's school reports stating: 'Bellamy is a good fellow, is maturing well but is academically useless'! However, just as ability comes in all shapes and sizes, so *there is no one certain method for recognising a very able pupil*. All have limitations, so it is important to use as wide a net as possible.

There are three other factors to bear in mind:

- relativity – i.e. a high achieving child in a high achieving school may be very different from one in a low achieving school;
- hostile environment – peer pressure or home background may not be conducive to success in learning, leading some children to under-achieve deliberately for fear of being labelled 'boffins' or 'swots';
- culture – children may have their talents masked in situations where there is a language difference.

Suitable identification procedures that your school could be using include:

- teacher observation and nomination;
- teacher assessments and statutory tests;
- pupil performance observation;
- parent observation and nomination;
- checklists of generic and subject characteristics;
- standardised achievement and intellectual ability tests.

Good teachers are sensitive, in their daily interactions, to the signals emitted by children in the classroom. Therefore, feelings based on your growing intuition and experience, plus the imaginative responses and the independence and insight shown by pupils as they go about their work are key pointers, despite the danger of subjectivity. The child may show particular commitment to a subject and an ability to go one step further than the rest. Individual discussion with able pupils will help you to note their articulation, depth of interest, vocabulary and flow of ideas.

It may be that signs are tangible: the child produces work of a consistently high standard, although it might mean the work you set is not demanding enough! You should also guard against rating pupils highly simply because they are tidy or industrious. Some bright pupils are superficially careless, so it is important to consider their underlying vocabulary, knowledge and conceptualisation. As your eye becomes increasingly trained, it should ensure you do not miss children who do not conform to accepted standards of behaviour or who present motivational or emotional problems.

Talking to parents about particular talents, interests and activities is an indicator because they often give their bright offspring strong backing, although their opinions can be over-optimistic. Clarke (1983) notes that other misleading clues include good home background, conformity, success of an older sibling, physical maturity, attractiveness and popularity. Conversely, *under*-expectation can occur with children from homes where there are low expectations, or with those who have motivational or emotional problems.

Checklists are an aid to recognising actual and potential high ability. They consist of distinguishing characteristics common to able pupils, which can then be used to check off against individuals. Scoring a large number provides an indication of brightness, although the total of ticks does not necessarily point to a child's level of ability. Pupils come in all shapes and sizes and differ in the traits they exhibit, so no single list can provide you with an exhaustive and infallible profile. Also, limitations on pupil–teacher contact time work against the use of checklists for accurate recognition.

Checklists used in teacher nominations fall into two categories:

- general signals one watches for from a pupil to indicate that he/she is bright;
- subject-specific characteristics showing what constitutes excellence in particular curriculum areas.

20 ways to spot bright pupils

- Sees humour in the unusual and absurd.
- Appreciates word humour – puns, nuances, word play.
- Demonstrates extensive general knowledge.
- Has a more than normal interest in serious items in the press and TV.
- Tends to speak like an adult in conversations.
- Challenges in an assertive manner during arguments.
- Prefers the company of adults to other children.
- Is a keen and alert observer.
- Has exceptional curiosity.
- Easily makes generalisations.
- Sees cause-and-effect relationships that are not recognised by peers.
- Quickly spots the direction of a story or situation.
- Displays pleasure and creativity in open-ended situations.
- Is skilful at working in the abstract.
- Exhibits intellectual playfulness, e.g. fantasises and manipulates ideas.
- Pays partial attention to explanations, but then copes easily with the work.
- Mental speed sometimes faster than physical capabilities.
- Reads rapidly and retains what is read.
- Capable of long periods of concentration.
- Has a hobby or interest which is followed to great depth.

(Based on Clarke 1983; Teare 1983)

A more able mathematician in a primary or secondary school may:

- display curiosity, imagination and flair
- calculate rapidly
- recognise pattern rapidly
- absorb knowledge
- grasp new ideas quickly
- extend tasks independently
- reason logically
- visualise spatial problems
- use own strategies
- pose own problems
- identify key issues
- omit steps when solving problems
- ask perceptive Maths questions
- transfer skills to other learning situations
- generalise from particular outcomes
- show a love for Maths

(National Association for Able Children in Education)

Aids to more systematic identification that should be available to you include records from children's previous schools, screening tests (e.g. the NFER Cognitive Abilities Test) taken on entry to their present school, IQ tests and school assessment and exam data. There is a problem, however, in drawing too general a conclusion from individual tests, since they may involve a specific and narrow definition of ability. The other worry concerns margins of error and variations in performance: quantifying results enables tests to take on an accuracy that is not always justifiable. It is common sense that the wider the testing procedure, the more reliable the conclusions which can be drawn about talent in different areas. Creativity is one area of imaginative or divergent thinking that is very difficult to define and assess objectively by conventional testing.

Once able pupils have been identified, their performance needs to be continuously monitored to ensure they benefit from their work. Teare (1983) suggests schools establish a 'shadow' SEN Code of Practice for this purpose, perhaps with a designated post-holder coordinating it. Certainly, teachers should use assessments that focus on the ability and skills displayed by bright pupils. This will be more relevant than rewarding reams of regurgitated information and will serve a diagnostic function. Some form of central record keeping system will enable decisions to be taken about future provision.

French checklist

- *Attitude* – shows enthusiasm for the study of French; perceives the subject as relevant to own future needs; shows active interest in learning about French way of life and the life of foreign countries in general.
- *Aural/oral skills* – able to discriminate between foreign sounds; able to articulate foreign sounds.
- *Oral response* – alert oral response to questions in French.
- *Control over sound/symbol correspondence* – pronunciation not perverted by written form of language.
- *Self-confidence* – not embarrassed when speaking French; enjoys trying out French sounds.
- *Memory* – shows clear evidence of good memory.
- *Mastery of English* – knowledgeable of essential grammar, e.g. parts of speech; alert to nuances of own language.
- *Flexibility* – can adapt to an entirely new set of rules and can think within them; does not try to impose English style or syntax on French sentences when writing compositions.
- *Ability to put the language together* – independently makes new connections out of isolated units of knowledge; makes creative use of French structures.

(Denton and Postlethwaite 1985)

✎ **Activity 11.1**

Think of several very able children in your classes and identify five characteristics for each one.
Compare them with the characteristics cited in this section. Discuss any similarities and differences with your induction tutor.

Curriculum provision

Eyre (1995) argues that schools can stimulate able children by adding more extension (depth) and more enrichment (breadth) to the core of the curriculum. This will enable them to learn widely, broaden the base of their experience and explore new ideas. Such enhancements should be built into differentiated schemes of work so that they form an integral part of the pupils' ongoing classroom experiences and enable them to study at a faster pace and a greater depth. If your school makes suitable curriculum provision of this nature, it will support you in encouraging the use of high level skills or creative responses. You should also offer open-ended tasks that allow pupils to develop knowledge and skills beyond the level normally expected.

Providing for extension in homework is a useful strategy, involving tasks that demand more thoughtful and research-based activities. So is exploring enrichment activities at lunchtime, after school, on Saturday mornings or any other time. It is valuable to operate an open access policy with such initiatives in order to widen opportunities for all pupils and create a general atmosphere of high performance and expectation.

Examples of activities that alter the curriculum routine include:

- university Maths Saturday schools;
- intensive Modern Language workshop days;
- engineering/technology/industry/ICT roadshows;
- subject competitions and quizzes involving writing, posters, poetry, inventions;
- residential courses;
- theatre workshops;
- writers/artists/poets/musicians in residence;
- bringing local clubs and societies into school.

What else could be done? There are several other options.

Individual study guides could be used, where appropriate, because they cater for pupils with an idiosyncratic form of talent, or those with a deep interest in a topic. The advantage of supported self-study is that it gives able pupils some ownership of the organisation and completion of their work. You, as teacher, provide the groundwork and guide and encourage pupils to explore further.

In order to develop the potential of the most able, some schools offer a central enrichment programme, in addition to normal subjects. Bright pupils are able to cope with greater intellectual challenges than many of their peers, so this should lead to opportunities for fostering originality and imagination through problem-solving, decision-making, role-play, open-ended questions and situations, creative and critical thinking skills exercises, teaching elementary philosophy, competitions, etc. Bloom's Taxonomy offers a particularly helpful framework for developing higher-order thinking and learning, as do the de Bono CORT programmes.

Schools can also allow the most able to study at an accelerated pace, which is easier in the secondary phase where there are specialist teachers. In Years 9 and 10, for example, fast tracking to GCSE is a possibility, with modular Advanced courses being started in Year 11 if timetable constraints allow. Sir Ron Dearing's 1997 review of post-16 qualifications even suggested sixth formers might study degree-level Open University modules. However, before moving a bright child into a higher age group, the school must be sure he/she has the maturity and social skills to cope.

CASE STUDY
The enrichment programme at Blessed William Oldcorne
RC High School, Worcester

Programmes are developed on the following principles:

- intellectual challenge based on the quality rather than quantity of work
- self-direction and independence of thought and action
- opportunities for originality and imagination through problem-solving.

Brainstorming sessions – involving topics/ideas/challenges/problems that are cross-curricular, stimulating and intellectually demanding.

Philosophy – offered to develop thinking processes and ideas.

Latin – an introductory course in Y9 and an extra subject in KS4.

Competitions – areas offer them to pupils when and where appropriate.

Early examination entry – where appropriate in specific subject areas.

Use of computers and IT – links with other countries are in use.

Extracurricular clubs – provide an opportunity for gifted children to develop skills further, e.g. madrigal choir, chess club, extra Science.

Organisational strategies

Teachers can rearrange classrooms to allow for *group or independent working*. The advantage of group work is that it makes lessons more participative, thereby encouraging children to be confident in their oral work and to take on more challenges. Resources should be easily accessible.

Using *different types of grouping* can have an important influence on the way the curriculum is taught to able pupils. Tilsley (1992) is one of several authorities to argue that putting bright pupils in various groupings can provide them with the skills, competition and teamwork to develop their potential – so long as it does not unduly isolate them:

- *ability grouping* – most able children thrive from the stimulus of working with 'like minds';
- *mixed age grouping* – sometimes younger bright pupils may be helped by working with older ones doing more advanced tasks;
- *specific interest grouping* – working on an area of interest with others who share that interest can be highly motivating;
- *gender grouping* – very able girls sometimes feel constrained by the dominant, attention-seeking behaviour of some boys;
- *personality grouping* – introverted able children may be disadvantaged by more gregarious, outgoing pupils.

If very able children are taught in *mixed ability groups*, there must be differentiated and challenging provision for the wider range in talent. It can be a daunting task, given limitations to the efficiency of the mixed ability approach. Kerry (1981) succinctly lists the pitfalls:

- teachers spend too much time with the slower learners;
- bright pupils can get away with not working at a fast pace;
- they fail to cover enough subject content;
- teacher delivery tends to be aimed at the middle.

If you are faced with mixed ability grouping, therefore, you should ensure it does not imply mixed ability teaching. More stimulating tasks must be provided for bright pupils within discrete groups if they are not to be under-challenged. Creating *withdrawal groups* for specific activities or topics is an alternative approach. Freeman (1997) states that American research indicates the benefits are most valuable in terms of self-confidence and more positive attitudes towards schoolwork. However, this kind of strategy is expensive in terms of teacher time unless specifically timetabled.

No one system of grouping, in itself, is more helpful to the able than another. The above examples offer valuable supplements for a curriculum that has the right degree of breadth, depth and pace. Stimulating teaching and learning experiences are important, too, as the next section explains.

Teaching methodology

Flexible and varied approaches are essential in teaching the most able. You should seek to develop use of a broad repertoire of open-ended tasks, group and individual learning, problem-solving activities and investigations. Doing this will enable you to match tasks to the variety in children's preferred learning styles. Active processes like these, involving guidance rather than instruction, enable bright pupils to:

- develop at least a partial responsibility for their own progress;
- learn to make decisions and solve problems; and
- work individually and cooperatively.

You should not be afraid of ensuring able pupils find work is challenging and difficult. OFSTED reports note that there is often a mismatch between teachers' expectations and what bright children can actually do. The pupils then learn to set their self-expectations too low. If tasks are too easy, they lose interest and enthusiasm, perhaps becoming a nuisance. It is vital to the pupils' personal development that they learn to cope with situations where, occasionally, they are unsuccessful. 'Over-load' is another problem. It is not the amount of work bright pupils do that matters, but the nature of the demand it makes upon them. Where you provide enrichment activities, they should be a substitute for – rather than a supplement to – the more routine aspects of a scheme of work. Repetition should be avoided, as these children usually need the least reinforcement, not the most.

Bright pupils need opportunities to *think*, rather than just 'do'. Tilsley (1992) observes that this does not always happen because of time pressures in completing programmes of study or the feeling that one must 'teach' all the time. Yet learning is an internal process that can work effectively only if there *is* time to think. So allow time for reflective thinking, using prompt questions like: 'What have you tried?' 'What else could you do?' 'What do you think about . . .?' 'What if . . .?' Also, able pupils should be offered a variety of means of recording work, e.g. letters, adverts, posters, oral work, dialogue, drama, diagrams, cartoons, video and cassette taping. Sometimes pupils develop and use processes that *we* have not thought of. This should not be discouraged.

The implication of all this for teachers of most able children is that they need to become more like enablers, guides and resource managers, by raising questions and offering challenges, encouraging the use of different learning activities, and providing a responsive environment. And to facilitate an effective and enriching teaching environment for the most able, there is a clear need for schools to ensure they accumulate a bank of suitable materials and resources. Libraries are an obvious base and locating them there should encourage independent learning and study outside lesson time. The use of ICT, such as CD-ROMs and the Internet, is another way.

The combined impact of all these strategies will bring benefits to pupils *outside* the definition of the most able. Children are not educated in isolation. Provision for the able should be carried out within the wider context of raising standards and enriching the education of *all* pupils.

✎ Activity 11.2

As a result of working through this section, you should now have a clearer idea of the attitudes, approaches and activities that will enhance provision for able and talented pupils in your classes.

Try undertaking a monitoring exercise on three bright pupils (if possible, of different ages) – over, say, a two week period – with a view to feeding back to your induction tutor responses to the following questions:

- How did you identify and recognise the display of ability and talent in your selected pupils?
- What have you done in your delivery of the curriculum to encourage high achievement by them, such as the use of extension activities or resources?
- What kind of organisational strategies have you employed in your classroom to improve their learning opportunities?
- Are you aware of their preferred learning styles and what have you done to respond to them in your teaching?

- What have you done to set thought-provoking homework?
- How have you assessed and monitored their progress on any extension activities you've set, including providing individual feedback?
- Have you rewarded any exceptional achievement by them?
- Have you made any communication with their parents?

References

Clarke, G. (1983) *Guidelines for the Recognition of Gifted Pupils.* York: Longman/Schools Council.

Denton, C. and Postlethwaite, K. (1985) *Able Children: Identifying Them in the Classroom.* London: NFER/Nelson.

DFE (1994) *Code of Practice on the Identification and Assessment of Special Educational Needs.* London: DFE.

Dickinson, P. (1982) *Could Do Better.* London: Arrow.

Eyre, D. (1995) *School Governors and More Able Children.* London: DfEE/NACE.

Freeman, J. (1997) 'Actualising talent: Implications for teachers and schools', *Support for Learning* **12**(2), 54–9.

Gardner, H. (1983) *Frames of Mind.* London: Fontana.

Gardner, H. (1991) *Creating Minds.* New York: The Free Press.

Kerry, T. (1981) *Teaching Bright Pupils in Mixed Ability Classes.* Basingstoke: Macmillan Education.

Ogilvie, E. (1973) *Gifted Children in Primary Schools.* London: Macmillan.

Teare, J. (1983) *Able Pupils: Practical Identification Strategies.* Oxford: NACE.

Tilsley, P. (1992) *Thinking About More Able Children In Your School.* Worcester: Hereford & Worcestershire County Council.

Part Two

Chapter 12

Lesson observations, reviews and target setting

Newly qualified teachers need regular assessment of – and feedback on – their teaching, their progress and the learning undertaken by their pupils. Informal, 'light-touch' observation and feedback will occur as part of the day-to-day discourse with induction tutors. However, a formal routine of observation and review is a process that has both formative and summative dimensions, as you will have found during your initial teacher training.

Making a diagnostic observation of your strengths (and any weaknesses) as a classroom/subject teacher – and, as a consequence, offering you ways to develop and enhance your knowledge, skills and understanding – is one of the most important responsibilities to fall on the shoulders of your induction tutor. Carrying out observations is also a crucial part of collecting evidence for your termly summative assessment meetings and reports.

Lesson observation, reviewing and target setting should be thought of as a cyclical process that includes:

1. Pre-lesson discussion between NQT and induction tutor.
2. The observation itself, so that important evidence can be collected.
3. A review discussion after the lesson in which the NQT receives feedback, offers comments and agrees on specific targets which could well provide a focus for the next observation cycle.

Underpinning the process is the need for developing a dialogue with your induction tutor, so that negotiation, consensual planning and co-analysis of practice occur. As you proceed through the induction year, it will help you to practise the skills of critical self-reflection that characterise the most advanced stage and lead naturally into further professional development. This element of self-evaluation should be introduced into your earliest observations, as it will support you in developing a self-evaluative approach to teaching.

Pre-lesson discussion

How you are observed needs careful negotiation and agreement in advance with your induction tutor, or whoever else undertakes this specific role, e.g. your school's SENCO, one of the senior staff or an advanced skills teacher. It is important to remember that observers tend to be different in:

- their own behaviour;
- what they choose to regard as important;
- the interpretation of findings.

So what are some of the key factors to take into consideration when planning and preparing for your observation?

The frequency of observation – During your ITT school placements, you were probably observed formally once a week. In the induction year, observation will not occur so often. A reasonable expectation would be once every four to six weeks, with the initial observation occurring within the first month of taking up your post. Although the frequency will often hinge on your competence and confidence, it should be sufficiently spaced to allow you time to demonstrate progress. To ensure a comprehensive picture is compiled of you, your induction tutor's observations should cover different teaching groups and different learning situations.

Establish the focus of observation – Your induction tutor will need to take into consideration your overall level of progress and the extent of your professional confidence. It is likely, for instance, that during the first half term you will be preoccupied with questions relating to your management and discipline of pupils. Further on in the year, once a purposeful working atmosphere is established, observations will concentrate on other professional standards relating to qualified teacher status, like:

- the encouragement of research work and independent learning;
- provision for the most able or SEN pupils;
- the presentation of key ideas and specialist terminology; or
- the use of questioning as a teaching technique.

The QTS and Induction Standards provide a useful bank of skills to draw on in identifying a primary focus for each observation. Your strengths and areas for development, as identified in your Career Entry Profile, comprise another tool. Having an agreed focus *is* important because it could be demoralising to be faced with a catalogue of skills and techniques on which you are going to be judged. Other skills can be tackled later, although that is not to say your induction tutor will ignore any other issues/problems that might arise if a lesson takes an unexpected direction.

Carefully plan the lesson – Your induction tutor will check to make sure you are adequately prepared. So make sure you:

- identify challenging but manageable learning outcomes;
- work out how they are to be achieved;
- intend to employ a sufficient degree of pace and direction;
- include differentiation or variety in your classroom organisation;
- relate your practice to specific teaching standards;
- adhere to the exam syllabus or scheme of work, etc.

Your observer will have to decide how to intervene at this point if it is felt there are any deficiencies in your planning. Or it may be that he/she has a different view of how a topic/task should be approached compared to your own assumptions or favoured practice.

Find out the timing of the post-observation briefing – The meeting should take place as soon as is practicable. You will be understandably anxious to glean from your induction tutor his/her opinion of the lesson. Also, the average school day is so hectic that your recollections could become a little fuzzy and your thoughts are likely to be overtaken by more immediate events.

Agree how the observation is to be carried out – Your observer needs to be aware of the effect of his/her presence in the classroom. Brooks and Sikes (1997) use the term 'researcher reflexivity' in addressing how – or whether, indeed, it is possible – to minimise the effect on 'normality' of having another person in the classroom. So how will you introduce your observer? Where should he/she sit?

One strategy is to tell pupils your observer has joined the lesson to see how well they are engaging in learning under your tuition and supervision. Your tutor can then sit unobtrusively at the back of the classroom. It also leaves him/her free to monitor and collect evidence. An alternative is active participation, especially with individual or group activities. This gives him/her greater insight into your planning and how far pupils understand what the work is about. However, getting too involved makes it difficult to observe methodically. Only in the most extreme situation will an observer seek to take a lesson over.

Videotaping parts of a lesson could be very helpful to you in seeing how pupils view your actions, gestures and movements. Children's work and their comments about what they learned or found difficult in lessons will provide your induction tutor with another rich source of evidence. Whatever form they take, records are essential to inform the follow-up discussion with your induction tutor and your termly summative assessment.

The observation itself

When the National Foundation for Educational Research investigated new teacher induction in the mid-1990s (Earley and Kinder 1994), it was found that lesson observations ranged from the formal (with agreed procedures) to the very informal – the latter being more common in primary schools. All the secondary NQTs interviewed could recount examples of formal observations by senior management or subject mentors. When mentors themselves were questioned, the time factor in organising observation and feedback was cited as a major difficulty – and it seemed to be middle managers who had most problems.

Since then, the increased use of lesson observation in school-based initial teacher training, appraisal and various forms of school self-review has strengthened awareness of its value in monitoring the quality of teaching and learning. Therefore, it is almost a dead certainty that your induction tutor will realise the importance of observing the *whole* lesson in order to get a clear idea of how you are progressing, rather than dropping in for a short while. Another reason is the very nature of classrooms as places of learning.

Beels and Powell (1994) make several telling points on this score. First, classrooms are *busy* places. Many decisions are made on the hoof rather than pre-planned. All teachers, even new ones, develop their own routines for handling classes. Classrooms are also *public* places. Teachers and pupils can feel as though they are 'on stage'. There is often a performance that teachers put on, especially in the way that some individual children are responded to. Then there is the fact that classrooms are *unpredictable* places. Unforeseen things can happen that teachers have to cope with. Internal and external disruptions and interruptions can occur. That is why it is important for your observer to be there for the *entire* lesson to get a clear picture of how all these things happen.

So how should your induction tutor conduct a lesson observation? The following represents some key aspects of good practice for anyone undertaking this role:

Good practice in lesson observation
- Ensure that others will not interrupt the lesson on your account.
- Arrive before the pupils enter the room.
- Sit outside the direct line of vision of the teacher.
- Ensure you can see all pupils.
- Adhere to the agreed focus and objectives.
- Strike a balance between the need to secure adequate written notes and the need to observe teacher and all pupils.
- Avoid participation unless you have arranged a participating partnership or agreed that talking with individual pupils would be helpful.
- Remain for the whole of the agreed session.
- Thank the mentee and give a very brief oral comment.
- Reflect and feedback.

(Acton *et al.* 1992, p. 22)

The type of recording procedure used by your school for observations is likely to have an influence on their conduct. There are at least three broad styles of observation schedule, each of which has implications for the way that lessons are evaluated. Discuss with your induction tutor the possibility of employing any of these different types, since their use is likely to prompt different types of professional discussion afterwards. A variety of approaches will also help you develop your skills of evaluation.

Open-ended observation schedules (see Figure 12.1) – These lead the observer to concentrate on making a detailed commentary under generic headings, like 'planning and preparation', 'classroom techniques' or 'professional qualities'.

Criteria-based observation schedules (see Figures 12.2a, b and c) – These specify sets of skills and competences against which lesson delivery can be assessed. This kind of observation instrument is more structured and has an obvious relevance to the current preoccupation with finely detailed teaching standards. The selection of a detailed focus for observation can be related to the particular stage of development an NQT is at during the induction year.

Pupil-centred observation schedules (see Figure 12.3) – These concentrate attention on the quality of children's teaching and learning experiences and their standards of achievement. Based on early OFSTED observation schedules, this approach is more suited for use later in the induction year when NQTs are less concerned with the minutiae of classroom practice and procedure.

Name:_____ Department:_____

Date & Lesson:_____ Year & Set:_____

Attributes	Comment
Planning and preparation	
Classroom techniques	
Professional qualities	
Additional comments	
Future targets	
NQT comments	

Signed:_____(NQT)

_____(Induction Tutor)

Date: _____

Figure 12.1 Open-ended observation schedule

Observation Focus 1: EFFECTIVE CLASSROOM MANAGEMENT

Name:_____ Department:_____

Date & Lesson:_____ Year Group & Set:_____

Indicators	Evidence-based judgements
Start and end of lesson	
Pupil entry to room and initial behaviour	
Teacher activity at the start of lesson	
Setting up/issuing/ collection of resources	
Knowledge of pupils' names	
Lay-out of furniture	
Tidiness of classroom	
Orderly ending of lesson	
Communication with pupils	
Tone, volume and pace of voice	
Effective questioning technique	
Clarity of explanations	
Awareness of individual pupils	
Use of black/white board	
Use of audio-visual aids	
Lesson structure	
Appropriate timing and phasing of lesson	
Suited to class ability and previous work	
Tasks broken down into small steps	
Maintains pupils' attention	

Figure 12.2a Criteria-based observation schedule

Indicators	Evidence-based judgements
Pupil behaviour	
Clear, consistent ground rules identified	
Pupils follow ground rules	
Watchfulness maintained on all parts of classroom	
Acts to pre-empt inappropriate behaviour	
Avoids confrontation	
Uses praise to promote positive attitudes	
Pupils sustain concentration	
Pupils are courteous	
Pupils work collaboratively	
Pupils show initiative and take responsibility	
Future targets	
NQT comments	

Signed:_____(NQT)

_____(Induction Tutor)

Date: _____

Figure 12.2a continued

Observation Focus 2: SUBJECT KNOWLEDGE, UNDERSTANDING & DELIVERY

Name:_____   Department:_____

Date & Lesson:_____   Year Group & Set:_____

Indicators	Evidence-based judgements
Subject knowledge and understanding	
Lesson content relates to KS3 PoS or KS4/5 exam syllabus	
Demonstrates knowledge and understanding of subject concepts/skills	
Builds on pupils' prior subject knowledge/skills	
Copes securely with pupils' subject-related questions	
Spots and remedies pupils' errors and misconceptions	
Subject planning and delivery	
Identifies clear objectives	
Presents key ideas, using specialist terms and well-chosen examples	
Sets challenging class/group/individual tasks	
Caters for special learning needs, e.g. SEN/high ability	
Stimulates curiosity and enthusiasm for subject	
Effective questioning	
Seeks to contribute to pupils' spiritual, moral and cultural development	
Appropriate use of texts, resources and ICT	

Figure 12.2b Criteria-based observation schedule

Indicators	Evidence-based judgements
Monitoring, assessment and recording	
Assesses achievement of learning objectives	
Relates assessment to AT levels/end-of-KS descriptions/GCSE grades	
Uses variety of assessment methods	
Marks pupils' work, gives constructive feedback and sets targets for progress	
Uses assessment data to inform future planning	
Keeps records of pupil progress in line with school/department policy	
Future targets	
NQT comments	

Signed:_____(NQT)

_____(Induction Tutor)

Date: _____

Figure 12.2b continued

Observation Focus 3: EFFECTIVE PUPIL LEARNING

Name:_____   Department:_____

Date & Lesson:_____   Year Group & Set:_____

Indicators	Evidence-based judgements
Individual pupil differences	
Shows knowledge of ways individual pupils learn best	
Matches subject matter and tasks to individuals' ability	
Creates opportunities to raise individual self-esteem	
Learning opportunities, goals and tasks	
Defines learning goals	
Offers learning activities relevant to learning goals	
Uses differentiated learning strategies for groups and individuals	
Challenges pupils' thinking	
Provides opportunities for pupil interaction	
Assesses whether pupils have met learning goals and provides constructive feedback	
Teaches individual and collaborative study skills	
Work environment	
Pupil seating/work place matched to learning activity	
Resources well organised and accessible	
Makes use of ICT	

Figure 12.2c Criteria-based observation schedule

Indicators	Evidence-based judgements
Effective communication	
Communicates learning objectives clearly and links to pupil activities	
Relates activities to previous/future learning	
Stimulates curiosity and enthusiasm for learning	
Communicates clear, sequenced instructions and expectations	
Makes effective use of questioning technique to provide pace and direction	
Listens to, analyses and responds to pupils	
Future targets	
NQT comments	

Signed:_____(NQT)

_____(Induction Tutor)

Date: _____

Figure 12.2c continued

NQT's name:_____Class:_____Date:_____
Content of lesson:_____
Quality of pupils' learning (e.g. attentiveness, concentration, interest, attitude, understanding of purpose of task and how to do it, work effectively, information seeking, communicating ideas and information, applying knowledge and understanding, complete tasks, make good progress, evaluate work)   Grade ____
Standard of pupils' achievement (e.g. quality of understanding, quality of written work, competence in key language skills, progress made in knowledge, understanding and skills, standard of work in relation to pupils' capabilities)   Grade ____
Quality of teaching (e.g. expectations of pupils, clarity of learning objectives, activities chosen to promote learning, assessment of understanding and progress, suitable pace of work)   Grade ____
Signed:_____Overall lesson grade_____
Key: VG = very good, G = good, S = satisfactory, U = unsatisfactory

(Furlong, J. *et al*. 1994, p. 62)

Figure 12.3 Pupil-centred observation schedule

Reviewing and target setting

Receiving constructive feedback on lesson observations is another very important entitlement for NQTs. It should not assume a secondary significance compared with the observation itself. You are being given information about your performance and its effect on the pupils, based on your induction tutor's accumulated professional and contextual knowledge. You are also being provided with a chance to feed your impressions back. It will enable you to pick up messages about how your observer feels towards you and what you are expected to achieve from the process.

That is why giving and receiving constructive feedback is a crucial skill for both induction tutors and NQTs. Acton *et al.* (1992) summarise its outcomes in terms of:

- leading to increased self-awareness;
- identifying options for alternative behaviour or further improvement;
- encouraging development.

The way in which the debriefing proceeds will depend, to some extent, on the stage of development you have reached. At the early stage, you will be focusing on classroom management, building up confidence and beginning to evaluate critically your own practice. So your induction tutor needs to ensure there is a balance between:

- giving feedback that is positive to build your confidence;
- advising on improving competence in a particular area;
- supporting self-evaluation.

Later, you can be challenged much more to set your own agenda and develop a more rigorous approach to self-evaluation. The ability to assume increasing responsibility for one's professional development is regarded by the DfEE as an important outcome of the induction year.

The following are some general pointers on successful debriefing based on good practice identified by Hagger *et al.* (1993) and the Teacher Training Agency (1999).

Where and when – It will be most helpful if your review meeting takes place at an early point after the observation – preferably within 24 to 48 hours. Allowing a little time to elapse will help you arrive at a more measured analysis and judgement of your lesson. Also, it should take place in an environment free of noise and interruptions.

Listening – You should be provided with an opportunity to take an active part in analysis of the lesson. Asking questions about your perceptions of the lesson will help your observer form an opinion about your capacity for reflecting on, and learning from, the experience, which he/she cannot possibly gain from an exclusive reliance on written feedback. So it is likely that the meeting will open with some general questions as a means of generating meaningful professional talk, e.g.:

- What is your view about how the lesson went?
- What do you think were its good points?
- Why did you do things in that way?
- Why do you think events developed in the way they did?

Accentuating the positive – Morale is a fragile plant in any teacher, not least NQTs. For many new teachers, the induction year is challenging, tiring and sometimes frustrating. Because it is easy for morale to take a knock, it is important for observers to find strengths and achievements in every lesson. Being too negative and critical will sap, rather than build, your confidence. For this reason, your induction tutor should separate you, the individual person, from any problem and keep critical comments impersonal. On the other hand, you do not want to be 'killed by kindness'!

So the aim should be to get the right balance between positive and negative comments. If a lesson has been a 'disaster', your observer should prioritise the key negative points. Less urgent issues can be returned to later. What is more important is to allow you to give *your* view of the lesson – and encourage you to identify and analyse specific aspects that could be improved. In this way, a spirit of open professional enquiry can be created. So far from it being a threatening exercise, you are actually encouraged to make helpful use of what is said. Feedback will be an easier, more enlightening experience when it is shown to be a collaborative undertaking, carried out in an honest and constructive spirit. As Brooks and Sikes (1997) point out, teaching is 'a career-long process of professional development and learning'.

Being concrete and specific – Sometimes, NQTs make sweeping statements about their lessons, e.g. 'it was fantastic/chaotic/dreadful'. Your induction tutor will need to give you guidance in assuming a more discriminating and analytical perspective about your classroom teaching. This process is helped if feedback relates to your agreed focus. Your observer should say exactly what you are doing and concentrate on specific actions and behaviour. He/she should refer to evidence, previously agreed criteria, what did or did not work well, and what can be changed or improved.

An agreed summary and targets for action – Agreeing with your induction tutor on a brief written record of the important points arising from your debriefing will help make sure you understand what has been said, and what now needs to be done. Needless to say, the written version should *not* be at variance with your oral feedback!

Target setting, of course, is the principal means of clarifying those aspects of your practice that require development. A target should be a clearly defined task that has been negotiated and agreed by both of you, rather than set and imposed by your tutor. Otherwise, it will not earn a high degree of commitment from you. A target should comprise a priority for development over a given period and should be clearly related to relevant QTS or Induction Standards. In short, it is a vital professional tool in the construction of an environment of self-evaluation and motivation.

What are the benefits of targets? Targets provide:
- a framework within which motivation can develop
- opportunities for the recognition of achievement
- strengthened collaboration and development
- an opportunity to prioritise tasks and ensure the best use of resources
- a clear focus for support, e.g. from other members of staff
- a link between self-development and organisational development
- an agreed written record of development
- a mode of working which should ease the transition into appraisal.

What is good practice in target setting? Good targets:
- have been negotiated...the outcome is a single agenda
- are of consequence and are closely related to a shared competency list
- make demands on both mentor and mentee
- are unambiguously stated in writing and are better described as 'aimed-for results' than activities...achievable in an agreed period of time
- possess agreed criteria for recognising success: objective criteria – relying on facts – or subjective criteria – relying on points of view
- can be codified or abandoned to suit changing circumstances.

(Acton *et al.* 1992, p. 80)

Activity 12.1

Ask your induction tutor to undertake a lesson observation with you during which he/she makes a detailed note of the specific learning experiences undertaken by an individual or group in the class – *without disclosing to you which pupil(s) are being monitored.*

After, find out which pupil(s) your tutor observed and give him/her an account of *your* perceptions of the individual/group's learning experiences. In exchanging your findings, concentrate on similar and dissimilar perceptions.

References

Acton, R., Kirkham, G. and Smith, P. (1992) *Mentoring: A Core Skills Pack.* Alsager: Crewe & Alsager College of Higher Education.

Beels, C. and Powell, D. (1994) *Mentoring with Newly Qualified Teachers – the Practical Guide.* Leeds: CCDU University of Leeds.

Brooks, V. and Sikes, P. (1997) *The Good Mentor Guide.* Buckingham: Open University Press.

Earley, P. and Kinder, K. (1994) *Initiation Rights. Effective induction practices for new teachers.* Slough: NFER.

Furlong, J. *et al.* (1994) *The Secondary Active Mentoring Programme 1: Principles and Processes.* Cambridge: Pearson.

Hagger, H., Burn, K. and McIntyre, D. (1993) *The School Mentor Handbook.* London: Kogan Page.

Teacher Training Agency (1999) *Supporting Induction Part 2: Support and Monitoring of Newly Qualified Teachers.* London: TTA.

Chapter 13

Assessing new teachers

The DfEE's Circular 5/99 deals at length with the statutory arrangements schools must follow for assessing NQTs, providing guidance on summative assessment meetings, the evidence to use for assessing progress and reporting procedures. There will be *three, termly formal assessment meetings* between you and your head teacher or the induction coordinator relating to your teaching and progress. These should have the following foci, although there might be adaptations depending on the pattern and rate of your progress:

> **Term 1:** Are you continuing to meet QTS Standards and beginning to address Induction Standards?
>
> **Term 2:** What progress are you making towards meeting the Induction Standards?
>
> **Term 3:** Have you demonstrated that you meet the requirements for satisfactory completion of induction? What objectives are set for your second year of teaching and longer term continuing professional development?

Documentary evidence to inform these meetings should be based on at least two observations and two progress review meetings, supported by specific pieces of evidence drawn from everyday teaching to show your progress and achievement, e.g.:

- lesson plans and evaluations;
- pupils' assessment data;
- information about liaison with colleagues and parents;
- evidence of your self-assessment and professional development.

Written records compiled by your induction tutor ought to be detailed in case there is any concern about unsatisfactory progress. All records should be available to you and your LEA, and must be retained in the event of any appeal process. The Circular provides templates for the documentation that has to be completed at each summative assessment meeting and then sent to the LEA, although schools and authorities may well make modifications. The Teacher Training Agency (1999) makes the explicit point that you should be clear about, and fully involved in, this assessment process.

The TTA is rightly confident that the vast majority of NQTs will have a successful induction into the profession. However, should you, by some unfortunate circumstance, be making *unsatisfactory progress*, you must be given early warning and any concerns communicated by your school to the LEA. The identification of any problems must not be left till the summative assessment meeting. In the event of your induction being at risk, your head teacher should observe you and put in writing the consequences of failure. The report on any NQT who makes poor progress should give details of:

- identified weaknesses
- agreed objectives

- planned support
- evidence on which the judgement is based.

Recommendations for passing/failing induction must be made to the LEA within 10 days of completing the final summative report. The LEA must respond within 20 days. Where a period of induction is extended (only in exceptional circumstances) or an NQT is deemed to have failed, details must be given of the right to appeal, currently to the Secretary of State and, soon, the newly established General Teaching Council. NQTs who appeal against failing induction must be dismissed or employed on restricted duties (as things stand, they cannot teach a class or subject in their own right).

So much for the nuts and bolts of the statutory requirements. The remainder of this chapter focuses on four essential and positive aspects of the assessment of newly qualified teachers:

1. Some guiding principles of NQT assessment
2. Using the QTS and Induction Standards
3. NQT self-assessment
4. Supporting NQTs 'at risk'.

Some guiding principles of NQT assessment

There are several key principles that should underpin the way your school approaches your assessment during induction.

- It should provide a variety of contexts and settings in which you can demonstrate your developing competence as a new teacher.
- The criteria for assessing you should not be a 'state secret'. They should be shared and agreed in advance so that you are fully conversant with them.
- The induction coordinator has a responsibility to ensure assessment criteria and procedures are applied consistently to you and any other NQTs in your school.
- There are important formative, as well as summative, aspects to your assessment, just as these two dimensions underpin the assessment of pupils. That is where, for instance, professional review meetings, lesson observations and target setting will be very useful.
- Your induction tutor should not see him/herself as the 'Lone Ranger' of assessment. The views and opinions of anybody else who is likely to have a worthwhile input to make should be invited, e.g. your year head or the SENCO, in order to gain an all-round view of your performance. He/she might even ask some pupils – very diplomatically – how you are getting on!
- There should be opportunities for you to engage in self-assessment throughout the year, linked to the review meetings with your induction tutor.
- Finally, the DfEE's new induction arrangements provide a cutting edge to how schools formally assess new teachers. Their professional futures will depend on the reliability and validity of how it is done. That is why your school *must* ensure procedures are robust, but also fair, transparent and objective.

Using the QTS and Induction Standards

In 1997, the Teacher Training Agency's *Standards for the Award of Qualified Teacher Status* were introduced. This meant that PGCE students seeking QTS, from then on, had to achieve *all* the Standards. From September 1999, this has extended to NQTs in the first term of their induction year, although Circular 5/99 talks about schools making a *judgement*, rather than a detailed re-assessment, based on the NQT's overall performance. The QTS Standards are complemented by the new *Induction Standards*, which are fewer in number and cover broader areas. These are the criteria against which your induction tutor must regularly monitor and assess you throughout your first year of teaching.

The Standards are intended to be precise, component statements that describe what effective performance means in a specific occupational context. Their use implies that student and novice teachers can be 'trained' to perform particular tasks and develop particular forms of behaviour in the most effective way possible. They are essentially behaviourist and product-oriented in approach. They have been formulated in such a way that they are meant to *build on and progress beyond* the QTS Standards. They should also offer scope for independent and prolonged displays of competence. Although these additional Standards do not refer specifically to subject knowledge, the TTA (1999) maintains that each one implicitly requires induction tutors to think about an NQT's *application* of subject knowledge.

The idea underlying the use of Standards is that they can be incorporated into a vocational qualification (Qualified Teacher Status) and inform the programmes of learning (PGCE course/NQT induction) that deliver them. Assessment processes, therefore, should seek to match the performance of individuals to the Standards by directly assessing/measuring them in work activities. That is why they comprise the first in a series of standards and qualifications, stretching through:

- advanced skills teaching
- subject leadership
- SENCOs, to
- headship (NPQH) and, most recently,
- the performance pay threshold.

There are pros and cons to this current fashion for a Standards-based approach to teacher education and induction. The *advantages* are that Standards:

- clearly specify desired outcomes in ITT and NQT induction;
- contribute to a consistent approach;
- provide a common entitlement;
- reduce the subjective element in assessment by permitting explicit evidence of progress to be gathered;
- get rid of the mystique from a teaching qualification and provide employing schools with knowledge of what to expect from NQTs;
- offer participants clear statements of target behaviour to aim for.

The *disadvantages* are that Standards:

- involve a narrow and mechanical approach, based on behaviour and skills;
- gloss over students'/NQTs' understanding of underlying concepts and questions like 'how', 'why' and 'when';
- encourage a checklist, MOT-test approach to assessment;
- undermine the development of a *gestalt* sense of professionalism – the whole is more than the sum of many parts.

Whatever the rights and wrongs of this task-based, utilitarian approach – with its emphasis on 'training' rather than 'education' – there are some important underlying issues to consider. McCulloch (1994) has summarised them in the following terms, although she was writing in the context of initial teacher training:

- First, induction tutors need to provide their NQTs with some triggers – some prompts, some hints, some clarifications – if they are to achieve success in performing tasks. The psychologist Vygotsky (1962) talked in terms of 'proximal development', i.e. the gap between one's present level of development and one's *potential* level, based on what could be done so long as help is provided. This suggests use of a form of assessment that attempts to measure the strengths of NQTs – what they can do in the best possible circumstances – as opposed to their failings.
- Second, there is the question of how far Standards based on classroom performance offer conclusions or judgements about an NQT's levels of *understanding*. There is a danger that exclusive use of an observable Standards approach may not satisfactorily address other elements in the complex process that we call education – unless, of course, observations are linked to meaningful, follow-up review meetings that dissect and explore the learning experience that NQTs are undergoing.
- Third, there is the implication in the use of Standards of a minimum acceptable level of performance, whereby NQTs simply pass or fail, rather than be placed on a *continuum* that stretches from no proficiency to excellent performance. The latter approach offers the potential to distinguish between 'novice' or 'threshold' competence and a 'superior', 'advanced' or 'higher order' level.
- Fourth, assessing NQT competence is sometimes an arbitrary, complex and unclear business.

To sum up, there are several important considerations that your induction tutor will need to bear in mind when using the Standards. These involve:

- applying the Standards diagnostically, as well as judgementally, in order to help you realise your potential for development;
- permitting you to demonstrate your capacity for learning and understanding in different tasks and situations;
- reflecting differences in levels of competent performance;
- recognising contextual or situational influences on your performance and taking these into consideration when assessing competence.

Table 13.1 Summary of the Standards for the Award of Qualified Teacher Status

A.	SUBJECT KNOWLEDGE AND UNDERSTANDING
1.	*Secondary*
i.	Know and understand concepts and skills in their specialist subject to degree level
ii.	Have detailed knowledge of NC programmes of study, level or end-of-key stage descriptions
iii.	For RE specialists, have a detailed knowledge of the Model Syllabus
iv.	Be familiar with KS4 and post-16 exam courses, including vocational ones
v.	Understand the framework and progression routes of 14–19 qualifications
vi.	Understand progression from KS2 programmes of study
vii.	Know and teach key skills required for current qualifications
viii.	Cope with pupils' subject-related questions
ix.	Know about and access inspection and research evidence
x.	Know pupils' most common misconceptions and mistakes
xi.	See how pupils' physical, intellectual, emotion and social development affects learning
xii.	Have a working knowledge of ICT up to level 8
xiii.	Be familiar with health and safety requirements
2.	*Primary*
i.	Understand purposes, scope, structure and balance of NC; aware of breadth of content of NC
ii.	See how pupils' physical, intellectual, emotion and social development affects learning
iii.	Have detailed knowledge of NC programmes of study, level or end-of-key stage descriptions
iv.	For RE specialists, have a detailed knowledge of the Model Syllabus
v.	Cope with pupils' subject-related questions
vi.	Understand progression through KS1 and KS2 to KS3
vii.	Be aware of inspection and research evidence
viii.	Know pupils' most common mistakes
ix.	Have a knowledge of ICT
x.	Be familiar with health and safety requirements
xi.	Have a secure knowledge of content specified in ITT primary English, Maths and Science
xii.	Have a knowledge of their specialist subjects to A-level standard
xiii.	Have a knowledge of non-specialist subjects to at least level 7 of NC
B.	PLANNING, TEACHING AND CLASS MANAGEMENT
1.	*Planning*
i.	Plan their teaching to achieve progression in pupils' learning through: • Identifying clear teaching objectives and content • Setting class, group and individual tasks which challenge pupils, including homework • Setting appropriate and demanding expectations • Setting clear learning targets built on prior attainment • Identifying SEN pupils, the very able and those with English difficulties

ii.	Provide structured lessons with pace, motivation and challenge
iii.	Make effective use of assessment information
iv.	Contribute to pupils' personal, spiritual, moral, social and cultural development
v.	Cover exam syllabi and NC programmes of study
2.	***Teaching and class management***
i.	Ensure effective teaching of whole classes, groups and individuals
ii.	Ensure sound learning and discipline
iii.	Establish a purposeful working atmosphere
iv.	Set high expectations for behaviour and use well-focused teaching to maintain discipline
v.	Establish a safe learning environment
vi.	Use teaching methods that keep all pupils engaged through: • Stimulating intellectual curiosity and fostering pupils' enthusiasm for the subject • Matching approaches used to subject material and pupils • Structuring information well as the lesson progresses • Presenting key ideas, using specialist vocabulary and well-chosen examples • Giving clear instruction and well-paced explanation • Effective questioning to provide pace and direction • Spotting and remedying pupils' errors and misconceptions • Listening to, analysing and responding to pupils • Selecting and making good use of textbooks, ICT and other resources for learning • Providing opportunities to consolidate and develop pupils' knowledge • Improving pupils' literacy, numeracy, ICT and study skills • Contributing to pupils' personal, spiritual, moral, social and cultural development • Setting high expectations, whatever pupils' gender, cultural or linguistic backgrounds • Relating pupils' learning to real and work-related examples
vii.	Familiar with SEN Code of Practice
viii.	Ensure pupils gain subject knowledge, skills and understanding
ix.	Evaluate critically one's teaching
C.	**MONITORING, ASSESSMENT, RECORDING, REPORTING AND ACCOUNTABILITY**
i.	Assess achievement of learning objectives and use to improve aspects of teaching
ii.	Mark pupils' work, give constructive oral and written feedback and set targets for progress
iii.	Assess and record pupil progress through observation, questioning, testing and marking to: • Check work is understood and completed • Monitor strengths and weaknesses for intervention in pupils' learning • Inform planning • Check pupils make clear progress in subject knowledge, skills and understanding
iv.	Be familiar with statutory assessment and reporting, and write informative parent reports
v.	Understand demands of level or end-of-key stage descriptions and KS4 and post-16 courses
vi.	Implement assessment requirements for 14–19 courses
vii.	Recognise levels of pupils' achievement and assesses against attainment targets
viii.	Know how assessment data can be used to set targets for pupils' achievement
ix.	Use variety of assessments for different purposes

D.	OTHER PROFESSIONAL REQUIREMENTS
i.	Know duties set out in School Teachers' Pay and Conditions Act 1991
ii.	Know legal responsibilities regarding health and safety, pupil care, discrimination, child protection and pupil sanctions
iii.	Build effective working relationships with staff
iv.	Set good example to pupils by presentation and conduct
v.	Be committed to maximising pupil opportunities and expectations
vi.	Take responsibility for own professional development and keep abreast of research
vii.	Understand responsibility for implementing school policies, e.g. bullying
viii.	Recognise need for liaison with parents, carers and welfare agencies
ix.	Aware of role of governors

> Primary teachers must also demonstrate that they know and understand teaching and assessment methods specified for primary ITT English, Maths and Science.

Table 13.2 Induction Standards

A.	PLANNING, TEACHING AND CLASS MANAGEMENT
i.	Sets clear targets for improvement of pupils' achievement, monitors pupils' progress towards those targets and uses appropriate teaching strategies in the light of this including, where appropriate, in relation to literacy, numeracy and other school targets
ii.	Plans effectively to ensure pupils have the opportunity to meet their potential, notwithstanding differences of race and gender, and taking into account the needs of pupils who are under-achieving, very able or not yet fluent in English, making use of relevant information and specialist help where available
iii.	Secures a good standard of pupil behaviour in the classroom through establishing appropriate rules and high expectations of discipline which pupils respect, acting to pre-empt inappropriate behaviour, and dealing with inappropriate behaviour within the behaviour policy of the school
iv.	Where applicable, plans effectively to meet the needs of SEN pupils and, in collaboration with the SENCO, makes an appropriate contribution to the preparation, implementation, monitoring and review of Individual Education Plans
v.	Takes account of ethnic and cultural diversity to enrich the curriculum and raise achievement
B.	MONITORING, ASSESSMENT, RECORDING, REPORTING & ACCOUNTABILITY
i.	Recognises the level that a pupil is achieving and makes accurate assessments, independently, against attainment targets, where applicable, and performance levels associated with other tests or qualifications relevant to the subject(s) or phase(s) taught
ii.	Liaises effectively with pupils' parents/carers through informative oral and written reports on pupils' progress and achievements, discussing appropriate targets, and encouraging them to support their children's learning, behaviour and progress

C.	OTHER PROFESSIONAL REQUIREMENTS
i.	Where applicable, deploys support staff and other adults effectively in the classroom involving them, where appropriate, in the planning and management of pupils' learning
ii.	Takes responsibility for implementing school policies and practices, including those dealing with bullying and racial harassment
iii.	Takes responsibility for their own professional development, setting targets for improvements, and taking action to keep up-to-date with research and developments in pedagogy and in the subject(s) they teach

NQT self-assessment

One valuable approach is to give newly qualified teachers some ownership of the assessment process via structured opportunities for *self*-assessment. By using the strength of the mentoring relationship to guide you through any critical points that might need to be made, it can help bridge the gap between the induction tutor's monitoring role and the more supportive and developmental aspects of such work.

Self-assessment has its limitations. Your evaluation of your developing competence will necessarily be framed according to:

- your particular (and possibly limited) understanding of teaching and learning;
- the perceived expectations of your induction tutor;
- your capacity for critical analysis;
- any difficulty you experience in acknowledging your strengths and, in particular, your weaknesses.

Brooks and Sikes (1997) draw attention to another issue: the fact that novice teachers are at the 'sharp end of the conflict between formative and summative assessment'. What this point means is that you may feel reluctant to take part in the kind of frank exchange with your induction tutor which self-assessment encourages because that person also has a judgemental role in deciding how successfully you have coped with induction. Nevertheless, you *can* be helped to make evaluations of your progress and attainment. If you are centrally involved in your assessment, you are more likely to feel a sense of commitment to developing your professional competence and understanding as you progress through your career. It is a particularly valuable and appropriate means of identifying the progress, and responding to the training needs, of adult learners.

So what practical steps could you be taking in this direction? Chapter 15 explores ways in which a substantial reflective practitioner approach can be developed. This section concentrates on a more specific and limited exercise.

You will have started your first post already familiar with opportunities for self-assessment that you gained during your PGCE school placements. You will also have had the experience of completing the first part of your *Career Entry Profile* before taking up your appointment. So there may well be value in creating for yourself, in cooperation with your induction tutor, a structured opportunity to complete a self-assessment schedule, based on the Induction Standards.

Figure 13.1 gives an idea of what part of it could look like. The example shown takes the Standard on pupil behaviour and breaks it down into a number of strands. What you could profitably do is think about your performance against these various strands and put ticks in the appropriate column. A comment could be added in the space underneath. You could then take it along to a professional review meeting with your induction tutor and use it as one of the bases for discussion about the progress you are making, along with other types of evidence like lesson observations and examples of pupils' work.

INDUCTION STANDARD: *Secures a good standard of pupil behaviour in the classroom*	1	2	3
Ensures beginnings and endings of lesson, and transition from one activity to another, are orderly			
Has clear, consistent ground rules which pupils understand, respect and follow			
Maintains watchful eye on pupils in all parts of classroom			
Acts to pre-empt inappropriate behaviour			
Avoids confrontation			
Uses praise and encouragement to promote positive attitudes			
Key: *1 = Very good 2 = Satisfactory 3 = Needs improvement*			
Comments and future target			

Figure 13.1 Self-assessment using Induction Standards

Needless to say, you would not aim to review your progress each time against every single Induction Standard. That way lies unmanageable bureaucracy. The benefit lies in the 'ownership' and involvement it extends – the process offers a valuable antidote to passivity in learning. You may also gain by seeing teaching and learning in greater complexity – that could actually be evidence of progress on your part. What is more, it provides a valid basis for helping you to identify challenging, but attainable, targets for the subsequent four weeks or so, and explore how these might be achieved. Taking a lead in furthering your own professional development, don't forget, is regarded by both the DfEE and TTA as one of the key outcomes of the induction year.

Other ideas for self-assessment activities, suggested by the TTA (1999), include:

- logging of 'critical incidents' or 'classroom snapshots' in relation to an area that has been identified for improvement;
- close observation of a few individual pupils and their progress;
- review and analysis of written evaluations of lessons that have been made over the course of a term;
- examining the work of a group of pupils in comparison with their work in other subjects.

Supporting NQTs 'at risk'

Finally, we come to the 64,000-dollar question: what can or should schools do to support an NQT who *doesn't* shape up during the induction year?

The theory is simple, of course. The QTS Standards are so rigorous that if a PGCE student passes muster on them, he/she should *not* fail to meet the Standards encountered in the induction year – especially with the targeted support and guidance of an induction tutor. Nevertheless, there *will* be a small minority of NQTs who make unsatisfactory progress. So schools should now have systems in place that will ensure:

- early warning of any difficulties
- pre-emptive action to help potentially-failing NQTs.

If such a strategy is codified in terms of an 'at risk' section in a school's policy document on induction, it will put a mechanism of targeted support in place that is explicit, effective and prompt. It will also ensure no one is in any doubt about what needs to be done or what their entitlement is, particularly in the event of any appeals to the LEA or the new GTC.

So what sort of things *could* go wrong? If an NQT has difficulties, they usually arise in the following areas:

- ineffective classroom control;
- an inability to establish oneself as a 'presence' with children;
- inappropriate teaching and learning activities;
- weak subject knowledge and understanding.

Many NQTs who have problems early on do, eventually, reach a satisfactory level of competence as a result of targeted intervention, support and training. What strategy, therefore, should you expect your new school to have in place? The following Case Study sets out the steps taken by one secondary school.

References

Brooks, V. and Sikes, P. (1997) *The Good Mentor Guide*. Buckingham: Open University Press.

DfEE (1999) *The Induction Period for Newly Qualified Teachers*. Circular 5/99. London: DfEE.

McCulloch, M. (1994) 'Teacher competences and their assessment', in McCulloch, M. and Fidler, B. (eds) *Improving Initial Teacher Training?*, 129–40. London: Longman/BEMAS.

Teacher Training Agency (1999) *Supporting Induction Part 3: Assessment of the Newly Qualified Teacher*. London: TTA.

Vygotsky, L. (1962) *Thought and Language*. Cambridge, Mass.: MIT Press.

CASE STUDY

'At Risk' Procedure for NQTs/PGCE Students

If any NQTs or students encounter difficulties with their classroom management and subject delivery, there are various strategies that induction tutors and mentors can employ:

- diagnose the exact nature of the problem (e.g. too informal a relationship with classes) and give an understanding of why he/she is going wrong
- set agreed attainable targets for action, with specific and practical steps outlined for securing an improvement in practice
- when progress is made, commend the NQT/student's achievement
- be upbeat and optimistic about the prospects for making a satisfactory improvement, so that he/she does not develop a mind-set of failure
- be honest and above-board about any continuing difficulties, while still giving support, advice and direction
- use the technique of 'modelling', so the NQT/student can focus attention on particular aspects of teaching by observing more experienced colleagues elsewhere in the school or in other schools
- secure advice and support from LEA inspection/advisory staff
- encourage participation in INSET courses that relate to the specific area of difficulty
- maintain a documentary record of the difficulties encountered, how they are being addressed, and what support and counselling are being provided.

NQTs who make unsatisfactory progress must be given early warning and the school's concerns communicated to the LEA. Termly reports must give details of:

- identified weaknesses, backed by evidence
- agreed objectives and planned support.

Where there is prolonged unsatisfactory performance by a *student*, the University must be informed that he/she is at risk of failure.

The head teacher must observe an NQT at risk and give written warnings about failure. The LEA must ensure assessments are accurate and remedial steps have been taken to try to help a failing NQT improve.

The DfEE's induction arrangements require there to be 'a clean and clear judgement' on why an NQT has failed to meet statutory requirements and is no longer eligible to be employed as a teacher. Therefore, induction extensions are permitted only in exceptional circumstances.

NQTs who fail have a right of appeal to the Secretary of State (eventually the General Teaching Council). NQTs who appeal against failure must be dismissed or employed only on restricted duties (they cannot teach a class or subject in their own right).

If NQTs have concerns themselves, they should speak to the Induction Coordinator or head teacher. If necessary, contact will be made with the LEA link inspector.

(Induction and Mentoring Policy: Sneyd Community School, Walsall)

Chapter 14

Identifying individual training and development needs

The DfEE's induction arrangements and the support materials produced by the Teacher Training Agency place great emphasis on schools carrying out an individual needs analysis of NQTs' training and development needs. The TTA (1999) states this must be done accurately in order to:

- make the best use of NQTs' skills and abilities;
- build on their ITT to make sustained improvements in the quality of their teaching;
- make sure their professional development is supported right from the start.

Effective induction and mentoring means taking this kind of approach, since NQTs arrive in schools having had a *range of different experiences*. While many will enter employment straight from school and university, some will have done teaching or youth work in one form or another:

- in a previous career (e.g. training personnel);
- as a pastime (e.g. sports/music/Sunday school);
- within the family by bringing up children.

Brooks and Sikes (1997) stress that one type of induction provision, therefore, will not fit everyone. Probably, some tailoring will be needed if you, as an individual NQT, are to reach your potential. Just as teachers match their pedagogical style and lesson content to pupils' individual learning needs, so that principle should apply to the work of induction tutors with novice teachers. That's why your new school should involve you in planning your induction. The *Career Entry Profile* is a significant step forward by virtue of the encouragement it gives induction tutors to match development and training to identifiable individual needs.

Another point about differentiated provision is that *NQTs' needs differ at particular points* in time during induction. They are not neatly compartmentalised, since the stage of development that a teacher is at will vary from person to person and term to term. So development needs must be interpreted flexibly and sensitively. For some NQTs, the learning curve will extend naturally upwards, but for others it could be more erratic.

Tickle (1993) and Maynard and Furlong (1993) suggest that, initially, your needs will focus on your classroom survival and whether or not you are doing what your school expects. You will understandably put great store on effective classroom management and control, although you must be careful that this does not dominate your approach to teaching and learning activities. Later, you will gain confidence in managing pupils, while at the same time providing them with meaningful tasks.

Having found ways of teaching that 'work', you will then move beyond this level of competent performance to more uncharted territory. This is likely to involve you focusing on issues about the curriculum, teaching and learning. It will lead you to:

- address the Induction Standards in a systematic way;
- develop your subject knowledge, understanding and delivery;
- explore ways in which pupils can learn effectively.

In making this transition, the active guidance and support of your induction tutor will be essential. That is why the induction and mentoring provision made for NQTs in their first schools *must* start from where they are as learners, and then take their individual patterns of development into account.

In terms of the *techniques* your induction tutor should be employing to identify and assess your individual training and development needs, five key approaches stand out:

- *use of the Career Entry Profile* to help move you from where you are currently to where you ought to be (see next section);
- *observation of classroom practice*, involving a preliminary meeting to agree criteria, the observation itself (with a specific focus) and a review meeting to discuss issues and use them as the basis for defining further needs;
- *professional review meetings*, in which you take a broader view of your development by discussing your achievements, your performance within the context of the Standards and your opinions about the value of your support programme – coupled with use of some kind of self-reflective profile or logbook;
- *reflective mentoring* based, where possible, on an active classroom teaching relationship between you and your induction tutor, whereby he/she acts as a reflective coach, as a critical friend or as a co-enquirer (see Table 14.1);
- *structured opportunities for critical self-reflection* undertaken by the NQT and focusing on an identified area of interest or concern, with the intention of informing and improving his/her professional practice (see Chapter 15).

Table 14.1 Reflective mentoring

Reflective coaching	NQT helped to think about and refine performance by an actively involved mentor who offers comments. Mentee's own professional experiences become basic material for learning about teaching, as mentor makes planned interventions to channel NQT's thinking.
Critical friend	Mentor challenges NQT to re-examine his/her teaching, while providing encouragement and support. Helps NQT shift focus from lessons as teaching opportunities for him/herself to how he/she can increase learning potential of pupils.
Co-enquirer	Priorities are negotiated, with NQT playing key role in identifying focus for attention. Observation and collaborative teaching are key techniques, with NQT taking lead in analysing/evaluating performance and using mentor's record as basis for discussion. Diagnostic assessment and prescriptions for action tackled collaboratively.

(Abridged from Brooks and Sikes 1997, pp. 23–8)

The remainder of this chapter focuses on the deployment of one particular strategy – the Career Entry Profile.

Career Entry Profiles

From September 1998, all newly qualified teachers have been required to have a Teacher Training Agency Career Entry Profile.

Profiling newly qualified teachers was first promoted in the early 1990s. Originally, a 'cradle-to-grave' system for teachers was envisaged, stretching from ITT through induction to further professional development, including appraisal. This picked up on a recommendation in an HMI survey (1988) that universities provide schools with profiles detailing students' strengths and weaknesses. Also, given the different routes people take into teaching, it was thought this would help schools to respond better to NQTs' individual needs. The idea has been revived by the DfEE (2000), with its suggestion that teachers have their own development portfolios, available on disk or the internet, in order to link training to career planning.

Purposes of the Career Entry Profile

The Profile will provide your school with baseline information about your strengths and priorities for further professional development, based on your PGCE performance. By virtue of the dialogue it creates, your induction tutor will be able to:

- deploy you effectively, taking into account your strengths and needs;
- devise an individualised induction plan based on your needs, whatever priorities your school has and any nationally identified initiatives;
- record and revise your agreed objectives and the action plan supporting them;
- provide you with targeted monitoring and support throughout induction.

As far as you are concerned, the Profile aims to help you:

- target and address your development needs and build on your strengths;
- make an active contribution to – and assume increasing responsibility for – your professional progress by target setting and reviewing, thereby establishing good practice that will later assist the performance management process and your future professional development.

Structure of the Career Entry Profile

The latest version of the Profile has three sections:

> **Section A** A summary of your college/university course.
>
> **Section B** An agreed statement of your strengths and priorities based on your performance during that course.
>
> **Section C** The key developmental section, where you and your induction tutor jointly engage in regular target setting and action planning for, and during, the induction year, based on the content of Section B, school priorities and national initiatives.

Using the Career Entry Profile

What process is your induction tutor likely to follow in using your Career Entry Profile? Here is one way forward:

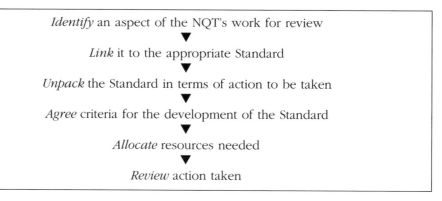

An *initial meeting* with you is needed to look at Sections A and B and discuss targets you have identified, complemented by any relevant priorities included in the school or department development plans, e.g.

- development of a GNVQ course;
- boosting number of high levels in KS2/3 SATs/TAs;
- incorporating use of IT into subject delivery.

This will require an investment in time on the part of your induction tutor in order to get to know you and discover what your needs are. Where you have worked out goals for the induction year – e.g. how to establish classroom control or the refinement of your questioning technique – it should give you more confidence about broaching such issues with your tutor. It is also likely to help you see that learning to teach is not just about 'doing', but *thinking* about doing.

The benefits for your induction tutor are that he/she will:

- more quickly locate any gaps in your knowledge, skills and experience;
- appreciate any assumptions you are making about your new role.

Once this is done, it is possible to agree on targets to address and link them to the QTS/Induction Standards. The relevant Standard(s) can then be unpacked in order to devise some practical and manageable ways to put the targets into action. Your induction tutor will probably need to negotiate the support of colleagues, such as subject staff, the ICT coordinator or the SENCO.

The next stage will involve your induction tutor:

- identifying specific criteria by which to evaluate the success of each target;
- calculating the resource implications;
- establishing deadline dates for reviewing and achieving your targets.

It is worth repeating that the exercise will require time and patience in order to negotiate and follow through, in view of:

- the need to set specifically short, medium and long-term objectives;
- the DfEE's requirement that the CEP is used as the mechanism for regular reviews of your professional development needs *throughout* the induction year.

Using the QTS and Induction Standards

As indicated above, the Career Entry Profile process must include the QTS and Induction Standards. Their role is to provide a 'menu' from which topics can be chosen that provide a 'best fit' for individual priority targets (see Table 14.2).

Table 14.2 Using QTS Standards to formulate CEP targets

SUBJECT KNOWLEDGE AND UNDERSTANDING			
TEACHING STANDARD	**ACTION TO BE TAKEN**	**SUCCESS CRITERIA**	**RESOURCES**
Detailed knowledge of NC programmes of study and level descriptions.	Relate statutory guidance to module in department scheme of work. Produce assessment mark scheme using levels. Put levels criteria into 'pupil-speak'.	Lesson plans take account of NC programme of study. Marking of pupils' work and teacher comments expressed in levels.	Time to work with subject mentor in relating module to NC PoS. Purchase teaching support materials tied into level descriptions.
Familiarity with vocational exam courses.	Visit another school offering GNVQ in subject area to gather information on subject delivery and forms of assessment employed.	Contributes to school's GNVQ programme. Lesson observation focuses on teaching process and/or forms of evidence used for assessment.	Day visit, followed by review of findings with subject head and/or vocational studies head.
Know about and can access inspection and research evidence.	Access OFSTED inspection reports on Internet. Join professional association for subject (e.g.Historical Association) and read journals. Study GCSE/A-level examiners' reports.	Awareness of recognised good practice in subject teaching. Keeps up-to-date with latest developments in subject. Advises pupils of good practice for exam questions.	School subscribes to Internet. Membership subscription for department staff. School library subscribes to journals. INSET on exam syllabus.
Working knowledge of ICT	ICT coordinator to run INSET session or work on consultancy basis in classroom. Observe good ICT practice in another department.	Ability to use appropriate hardware. Aware of software suitable for class use. Lesson plans show evidence of ICT, e.g. use of CD-ROM.	Time for INSET or use of coordinator in classroom. Purchase of software by department.

Table 14.2 continued

PLANNING, TEACHING AND CLASS MANAGEMENT			
TEACHING STANDARD	**ACTION TO BE TAKEN**	**SUCCESS CRITERIA**	**RESOURCES**
Identify clear teaching objectives and content.	Develop understanding of criteria for effective lesson planning. Understand variety of pupils' learning styles. Develop methods to assess pupils' success in meeting objectives.	Lesson plans define goals and demonstrate pace and progression. Teaching objectives are shared with pupils. Clear links between goals and teaching/ learning activities.	INSET on effective teaching and learning. Lesson observation and feedback by subject mentor.
Identify very able pupils.	Recognise generic and subject characteristics of able pupils. Awareness of suitable teaching methods, organisational strategies and curriculum provision.	Uses assessment data to identify able pupils in teaching sets. Focus on differentiated provision in lesson observations.	INSET on appropriate teaching, assessment and classroom management strategies. Lesson observation and feedback.
Set high expectations for behaviour and use well-focused teaching in order to maintain discipline.	Awareness of school policy and department procedures on behaviour. Observe good practice in school. Devise ground rules for classroom control.	Has ground rules for pupil conduct. Praises and encourages. Improved pupil–teacher relations. Demonstrates efficient planning and organisation.	INSET on positive behaviour management. Observation of more experienced colleagues who successfully promote positive behaviour.
Contribute to pupils' personal, spiritual, moral, social and cultural development.	Development of form tutor's role. Knowledge of pupils' variety of backgrounds. Familiarity with equal opportunities issues. Urge to view school as moral community.	Effectively fulfils form tutor's role. Demonstrates awareness of, and respect for, pupils as individuals. Lessons reflect opportunities equal issues. Extracurricular activities.	Meetings with PSE and Equal Opportunities Coordinators. Opportunity to explore links with external agencies and stakeholders.

Table 14.2 continued

MONITORING, ASSESSMENT, RECORDING AND REPORTING			
TEACHING STANDARD	**ACTION TO BE TAKEN**	**SUCCESS CRITERIA**	**RESOURCES**
Assess and record pupil progress through observation, questioning, testing and marking.	Provide a critical awareness of the wide range of formative and summative assessment techniques available. Identify and observe examples of good assessment and recording practice in school.	Lesson plans and observations show variety of formative and participatory assessments. Pupils' work shows regular marking and constructive . comments Keeps up-to-date records in line with departmental and school policy.	INSET with Assessment Coordinator on formative and summative assessment. Time for observation of good practice in different areas of school.
Familiar with statutory assessment and reporting, and writes informative parent reports.	Knowledge of current statutory requirements. Knowledge of school procedures for reporting.	Produces detailed and well presented school reports. Reports set targets for pupils and identify ways to plan action for improvement. Reports enlist parental support.	INSET involving critically reviewing examples of reports, practising report writing and dealing with parents at consultation evenings.
Recognises levels of pupils' achievement and assesses against attainment targets.	Develop awareness of what constitutes achievement at different levels of attainment or in end of Key Stage statements. Appreciates value and limitations of NC assessment tools.	Makes realistic assessments of pupils' progress in line with level or end-of-KS criteria. Translates levels/ descriptions into 'pupil-speak' to facilitate understanding. Uses assessment data as part of planning process for individuals.	Involvement in compiling departmental portfolios of exemplary work for assessing NC levels.

Table 14.2 continued

OTHER PROFESSIONAL REQUIREMENTS			
TEACHING STANDARD	**ACTION TO BE TAKEN**	**SUCCESS CRITERIA**	**RESOURCES**
Knows legal responsibilities about health and safety, pupil care, discrimination, child protection and sanctions.	Knowledge of appropriate legislation. Knowledge of school procedures for addressing legal responsibilities.	Demonstrates working knowledge of legal responsibilities and school procedures as classroom teacher and form tutor.	School handbook and policies. INSET on relevant topics, e.g. child protection, involving case studies.
Builds effective working relationships with staff.	Provide opportunities in meetings for expressing NQT views. Use NQT's strengths and interests to identify areas for contributing to school development.	Contributes effectively in departmental and pastoral team meetings. Takes part in project working parties.	Resources to support initiatives in which NQT is involved.
Takes responsibility for own professional development and keeps abreast of research.	Awareness of preferred career direction. Knowledge of suitable INSET to develop competence. Access to books and journals.	Commitment to developing professional competence. Ability to engage in professional debate on topical issues.	Meetings with senior mentor. Funding for INSET courses. Provision of educational journals and books in staff library.

For instance, you and your induction tutor might want to work on the management of pupil behaviour. Three germane QTS Standards are:

- ensuring sound learning and discipline
- establishing a purposeful working atmosphere
- setting high expectations for behaviour and use of well-focused teaching.

Also relevant is the Induction Standard on:

- establishing appropriate rules and high expectations of discipline
- pre-empting inappropriate behaviour
- use of the school's behaviour policy.

On that one issue alone, *both* sets of Standards provide a framework in which you can work and make progress, in collaboration with your induction tutor, on the *day-to-day* basis that Circular 5/99 recommends.

A note of caution should to be sounded here. Your aim must be to make progress in developing professional competence vis-à-vis your targets and the Standards. However, it is vital not to fall into the trap of thinking that achievement of the success criteria occurs on a 'once-and-for-all' basis. As stated earlier, the Standards should not be regarded as embodying benchmarks that you pass or fail like an MOT car test. They should lead you to look *beyond* 'competence', in a technical sense, to aim for gradations of performance that recognise the development of more sophisticated patterns of, and perspectives on, professional behaviour. So one important aim your induction tutor should have is to encourage you to regard your professional competence as a *continuum* – something that can be developed further in more challenging contexts or more complex ways *at any point* in your career.

Another vital point to realise is that the Standards share some common ground with each other and should not be treated in isolation. For example, establishing a purposeful working atmosphere (teaching and class management) cannot be considered in isolation from:

- setting challenging tasks (planning); or
- coping with pupils' subject-related questions (knowledge and understanding).

The Profile makes it clear that areas for concern *and strengths* should be explored. Taking an area of strength or enthusiasm will be useful in developing your confidence and maintaining professional interest. With any identified areas of difficulty, your induction tutor will find advantage in employing a *problem-solving* approach, whereby you are encouraged to look for, and contribute, your *own* answers to an analysis of the situation. At times, this will require your tutor to hold back on advice and demonstrate his/her ability to listen, thereby avoiding the imposition of quick-answer coping strategies.

Used in these ways, the Standards and the Profile should provide a flexible and valuable means of:

- giving you support during induction;
- responding effectively to your development and training needs.

References

Brooks, V. and Sikes, P. (1997) *The Good Mentor Guide*. Buckingham: Open University Press.

DfEE (2000) *Professional Development: Support for Teaching and Learning*. London: DfEE.

HMI (1988) *The New Teacher in School 1987*. London: HMSO.

Maynard, T. and Furlong, J. (1993) 'Learning to Teach and Models of Mentoring', in McIntyre, D., Hagger, H. and Wilkin, M (eds) *Mentoring: Perspectives on School-Based Teacher Education*, 69–85. London: Kogan Page.

Teacher Training Agency (1999) *Supporting Induction Part 2: Support and Monitoring of Newly Qualified Teachers*. London: TTA.

Tickle, L. (1993): 'The first year of teaching as a learning experience', in Bridges, D. and Kerry, T. (eds) *Developing Teachers Professionally*, 79–92. London: Routledge.

Chapter 15

Developing self-reflective practice

The QTS and Induction Standards have a valuable part to play in providing a suitable framework for induction. However, as a newly qualified teacher you should also engage in a scrutiny of your developing professional practice that extends beyond a purely skills-based model. The ethos and priorities of your school are important to this approach – and the key to its implementation is the encouragement of a problematic, reflective appraisal of your emerging teaching and learning practices.

This chapter offers ideas about creating opportunities for you to reflect actively and self-critically on aspects of your professional practice by considering:

1. The meanings attributed to 'reflective practice'
2. How action research can be used to improve your practice
3. How a structured reflective practice exercise can be undertaken
4. The main issues for your school in managing a reflective practice exercise.

The meanings attributed to 'reflective practice'

Put simply, 'reflective practice' is a practical enquiry undertaken for the purposes of understanding and improving one's professional practice. If this definition is unpacked, we can say:

- it entails offering new teachers a set of skills and strategies to integrate into their practice;
- it leads them to focus on relevant issues, with a view to seeking practical solutions and developing their personal understanding of relevant educational concerns;
- it involves them actively considering their emerging knowledge and values about teaching in terms of the grounds that support them and the consequences to which they could lead.

'Reflective practice' is a concept that has featured in the work of a number of educationalists. It can shift according to the concerns and the uses made of it.

John Dewey (1933) – He said reflective practitioners engage in active, persistent and careful consideration of any belief or knowledge. Such habits, dispositions and skills must be carefully nurtured and he stressed the importance of 'continuous formation'. By this, Dewey meant people are constantly participating in and reconstructing their professional experiences. There is a clear implication that induction tutors can help new teachers by assisting them to explore their developing sense of professional 'self' in relation to their actions in the classroom. There are echoes here of Jean-Paul Sartre's call for us to try to make ourselves what we *might* be.

Donald Cruikshank (1987) – For Cruikshank, reflective teaching is the ability to analyse one's own teaching practice through something akin to a structured, laboratory-type experiment. He worked with student teachers on the analysis of their teaching practice. It involved them identifying forms of teaching that research has judged to be effective and repeating it with a small group of fellow-students. Through discussion, they assessed how far their teaching had been successful. The emphasis was on applying theory to a classroom situation to make their technical practice more effective.

Donald Schön (1983, 1987) – He argued that we should look less to the work of researchers and more to the 'competency and artistry...embedded in skilful practice'. He said 'knowledge-in-action' is constructed – or reconstructed – from practice, which leads to 'reflection-in-action'. This involves thinking 'on one's feet' or 'in the thick of things', although he recognised it is impossible for the process to take place all the time. He also stated that one should 'reflect-*on*-action', i.e. stand outside the day-to-day world of the classroom in order to examine practice after the event or in other contexts. It is vital, of course, to be able to recognise what is problematic and then create a suitable context in which to respond. Schön called this process 'problem setting'. The purpose is to change a situation from where it was lacking to a more desirable state. He urged practitioners to learn from:

- what they do themselves;
- coaching by experts (in the case of NQTs, induction tutors fill this role);
- dialogue with other novices.

The views of Cruikshank and Schön place a strong emphasis on the teacher's technical practice in *doing* the job effectively. However, it does not extend to considering the broader contexts of educational goals or school structures.

Kenneth Zeichner (1987) – He said teaching and schooling need a reflective orientation that seeks to contribute to justice and equality. This will necessarily involve examining the aims, values and purposes of the educational system. That is why new teachers should go further than the immediate situation and imagine things as they *should* be. This takes 'reflective practice' beyond questions of 'doing the classroom job effectively' to goals embedded in teaching, the curriculum and the school structure itself.
Zeichner put forward three levels of reflection:

- the technical aspects of teaching, where the emphasis is on the efficient application of professional knowledge;
- its situational and institutional contexts, such as the values or assumptions that may be embedded in a school's norms;
- the underlying moral and ethical issues, whereby teachers examine the ways in which schooling generally, and one's own teaching specifically, contribute to justice and equality.

There is a clear implication in all this. Induction tutors should help NQTs to develop skills in classroom contexts, but it ought not to stop there. You should also be encouraged to develop an attitude of enquiry regarding your professional practice that leads you to think *critically*, not comfortably, about those contexts and their effects on the children who function within them. It should help you to ask questions that concentrate on imagining things as they ought to be, not simply accepting things as they are – that focus on the 'possible', rather than the 'existing'.

How action research can be used to improve your practice

If your school successfully creates opportunities for you – as an NQT – to engage in critical self-reflection, you will find yourself able to:

- define your own immediate issues or problems;
- work towards practical and specific solutions;
- reflect on your results and your viewpoints from a wider perspective.

This, in effect, is the *cycle of action research*. Like 'reflective practice', action research is a generic term that embraces a variety of strategies, all of which are designed to result in improvements in some practical situation. What action research does is offer a suitable vehicle for enabling new teachers to undertake four sequential activities:

- observe what is already happening;
- research what could be done to improve current practice;
- monitor the effects of the new action undertaken;
- reflect on these effects as a basis for further planning and action.

What is action research?

Action research is a form of self-reflective enquiry undertaken by participants (e.g. teachers, students or principals) in social (including educational) situations in order to improve the rationality and justice of:

- their own social or educational practices,
- their understanding of these practices, and
- the situations (and institutions) in which these practices are carried out.

(Carr and Kemmis 1986)

The cycle actually occurs as part-and-parcel of what good teachers are supposed to be doing anyway in their everyday work, i.e. being aware of their classroom practice and attempting to improve it. It involves doing self-consciously what should come naturally! What is different is that teachers engaged in action research carry out such activities in a more measured and systematic manner than normal, focusing on selected issues over a longer period of time. Furthermore, one's actual teaching constitutes much of the process of experimentation – it is not an isolated activity – in order to create a process of change and improvement of practice.

Probably that is why action research is an increasingly popular form of educational research. Its main focus is on involving teachers as participants in their own educational process and encouraging them to reflect on their practice. Applied to the classroom, it aims to improve education through change by encouraging teachers to be:

- aware of their practice in a particular situation;
- critical of that practice;
- prepared to change it.

Other important characteristics include:

- adopting a flexible trial-and-error approach;
- accepting one might not arrive at a final answer;
- aiming to ground any claims one makes firmly in one's observations and findings.

So action research is a participatory form of research, in that it involves the teacher in his/her own enquiry. It is also collaborative, because it concerns other people as part of a shared enquiry. It can be a search for questions as well as answers. It seeks to pose problems as well as solve them. Any claims or 'theories' generated are validated through practice. That is why action research is commonly regarded as a research method used consciously by good teachers to improve their practice.

The experiential learning model devised by Kolb and Fry (1975) provides a useful template for NQTs to use in collaboration with their induction tutors. They argued that if one wants to encourage learning, change and growth, it is done best via an integrated process that goes through four stages.

Stages one and two involve using immediate classroom experiences as the basis for observation and reflection. They are then assimilated in stage three into a 'theory' from which new implications for action can be worked out. In stage four, these serve as guides in creating new experiences that could be the focus for a further cycle of action and evaluation. The following diagram represents the process.

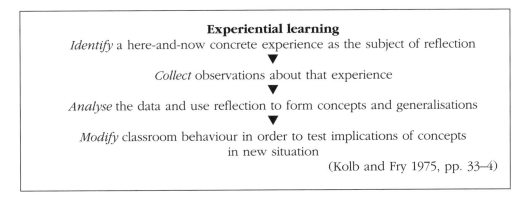

How a structured reflective practice exercise can be undertaken

Identify an area of professional interest or concern

Select an area of professional practice to act as your theme. You should discuss this with your induction tutor in one of your review meetings. The QTS and Induction Standards may well offer you an initial focus in the areas of:

- subject knowledge and understanding;
- planning, teaching and class management;
- monitoring, assessment, recording and reporting;
- other professional requirements.

Focus on one aspect that causes you interest or concern

Select one aspect or 'angle' that is professionally significant to you as an area of interest or improvement, e.g.

- Do I have high enough expectations of pupils of high ability in my Year 9 class?
- Does my teaching in Year 7 take sufficient account of the knowledge, skills and understanding that pupils have brought from Key Stage 2?
- Do I employ teaching methods which develop a style of independent learning?
- Do I give positive feedback to pupils in order to help them improve?
- Do I use appropriate strategies that encourage positive behaviour?

Consider what you think you can do about it

Having made an audit of your current practice, here you need to imagine possible ways in which your selected aspect of current practice can be changed or improved. You need to articulate your field of action by considering:

- What is my current practice like?
- Why is it like this?
- What precisely do I want to improve?
- Why is it professionally important to me?
- How could I go about this?
- What and/or whose assistance do I need?

Implement and monitor your strategy for improvement

Once you have a clear plan in mind, with some 'imagined solutions', you can translate it into manageable action. The action you take – your strategy for improvement – should be documented carefully, so make sure you keep a record of your action, such as lesson plans, a logbook, an audiotape or a video. Conversational evidence from pupils and departmental colleagues will also prove useful. This will provide you with data for your evaluation. During this time, you need to get your induction tutor to work with you as a 'critical friend' in order to raise questions in your mind and encourage you to explore the implications of your answers. You also need to develop your own powers of interpretation so that you are probing and moving beyond your existing thinking.

Evaluate your research evidence

This is where you reflect upon the outcomes of your action and work out an evaluation of its success. Questions to ask yourself and your induction tutor include:

- Has there been a practical change in my professional practice?
- Have they any significance, and for whom and why?
- Do I like them?
- What actual evidence supports my analysis?
- Is it sufficient or could it be strengthened?
- Have I engaged in a critical dialogue with any colleagues about my claim that improvement has taken place?
- Can I contextualise my findings in any educational literature?
- How far can my action be related to wider issues of morality and equality in education?
- Are there any constraints on my action, arising either within this school or in the education system on a wider level?
- Have I developed professionally as a consequence of this exercise?

Establishing a claim for improving professional practice

The final stage is to establish a claim about moving your professional practice forward in your chosen field of action. It involves you making a brief written report and presentation to your induction tutor, and any other NQTs in your school, about what you claim to have learned as a result of your action. You need to be *convincing* about your claim – hence the importance of evidence. You also need to be *critical* about the criteria you have used to make judgements about what you are claiming as an improvement. This sense of 'moving forward' is your reflection *on* action.

CASE STUDY

Self-Reflection in Practice

The reflective practice framework that I identified for my NQTs to follow was very similar to the Kolb and Fry model. I wanted each one to select an area of interest or concern, audit their current practice, form a concept about how that practice could be changed, and then implement, monitor and evaluate a strategy for improvement.

The exercise occupied six weeks in the second half of the 1997 autumn term, with the final week devoted to reflecting on the outcomes and establishing a written *Claim for Improving Professional Practice*. These formed the basis for an afternoon symposium in January, when the NQTs made short presentations and took part in an evaluation of the project's usefulness and its implications for professional development.

Although I suggested some background reading, I wanted them to use their own critical faculties to focus on a problem and raise questions about how to improve it. I had an initial 30-minute tutorial with each NQT to identify a broad area. We then focused on one aspect. This is what Schön calls 'problem setting', i.e. leading teachers through a process in which 'interactively we name things on which we will attend and frame the context in which we will attend to them'.

During the next six weeks, I liaised with the NQTs as a 'critical friend' to prompt questions and encourage them to recognise the implications of their answers. At the same time, I was keen to see how far they could develop their own interpretive resources in improving a chosen situation.

The reflective practice cycle I created for my NQTs went through the stages outlined on the following two pages. The topics chosen were:

- *developing positive attitudes to homework in a middle-band Y9 set*
- *encouraging positive attitudes to performance in mixed-ability PE*
- *differentiated activities for less able pupils in Y8 gymnastics*
- *a good behaviour strategy for a Y9 Music class*
- *positive oral feedback to accompany the marking of pupils' work.*

(Bleach 1998, pp. 7–15)

The main issues for your school in managing a reflective practice exercise

There are a number of key points relating to the *process* of reflective practice that school induction tutors should bear in mind when undertaking such an exercise with NQTs.

Choice of 'relevant' topic – In exploring potential topics, it is vital for your tutor to be aware of the concerns and priorities you will have at the start of your career. These often focus on practical issues, like behaviour, classroom organisation, pupil relationships and how best to excite interest and motivation. You will need help with formulating a focus that is motivating, challenging and practicable. Some issues may appear idealistic, so assistance may be needed in pinpointing a manageable target to aim for.

Time must be created – Sometimes you will feel swamped by the demands you face. Issues relating to educational theory and practice cannot be addressed during the lesson bell or in the exhausted half-hour at the end of a hectic day, so self-reflection will have little value if it is perceived by you as just another hurdle to surmount during induction. That is why it is important to:

- restrict the exercise to a limited time period;
- ensure you work with one class, or even a group of pupils within a class;
- create 'quality time' for a concluding presentation and evaluation.

Recording and monitoring – The 'action' in action research needs careful documentation. So keeping a log in which to note actions, incidents, reactions, frustrations and successes is necessary, even if it is difficult at times to monitor actions in the bustle of classroom activity.

Generalising from research outcomes – While recognising that they do not constitute 'final answers', the possibilities for improved practice that emerge from this kind of exercise have potential for more general application. Every situation researched will be specific to the pupils in question, yet your findings will constitute a data base that could be valuable for use with other classes and by other teachers.

Build on and develop pre-existing beliefs – It will be important for your induction tutor to encourage you to develop your own perspectives. Many NQTs feel obliged to make adjustments to the norms and expectations of their first school. However, this kind of exercise should generate space for welcoming individual contributions from new teachers and for nurturing new perspectives.

Be aware of emotional factors – Asking new teachers to inquire into their actions could lead to feelings of anxiety if the experience is negative. Yet it is important that your induction tutor helps you to develop an understanding of what is happening to you when professional challenges arise. You also need to realise both trial *and error* are necessary elements in any action research project.

Reflection within a group of supportive teachers – You will benefit from sharing with your colleagues your thoughts about the issues that you encountered. This reduces any sense of isolation you might have had in coping with challenges. They can become resources for you through professional dialogue and debate.

Good teachers have always spotted problems, weighed up alternative solutions, tried out their ideas, and then made a considered judgement about what amounts to good practice. It is precisely this ability to take stock of, and then respond to, the demands of a given situation in order to improve one's professional practice that reflective practice seeks to develop in NQTs.

It is advantageous to do this right from the start of your career. The first year of teaching offers great opportunities to engage in reflection *in* and *on* action because NQTs bring into their new schools their emerging ideas about teaching and learning. Induction permits them to build on their initial teacher training course by continuing to explore ways to teach and to develop an awareness of the kind of teacher they wish to be.

The specific benefits of this kind of exercise include:

- becoming more aware of your own developing teaching practice and of what your pupils are thinking and experiencing;
- gaining new insights into how pupils learn in the classroom;
- developing a sympathetic viewpoint towards practitioner research;
- sharpening your skills of critical analysis, particularly in terms of learning to base judgements on observable data;
- most important of all, you can pursue ways of *improving* on your existing practice.

Induction tutors, therefore, have a crucial role in providing structured support for new teachers to bring their ideas and actions out into the open and subject them to professional scrutiny. Hopefully, they will be laying the foundations for a career-long appraisal of classroom practices and beliefs, which is essential if teachers are to develop as creative, thinking professionals, and not remain mere functionaries. An intelligent professional, after all, is a person who is accustomed to reflecting on his/her practice, to regarding it as problematic and open to change, and to deliberating rather than asserting.

References

Bleach, K. (1998) 'Self-reflection: an aid to NQTs' practice', *Professional Development Today* **1**(3), 7–15.

Carr, W. and Kemmis, S. (1986) *Becoming Critical.* Lewes: Falmer Press.

Cruikshank, D. (1987) *Reflective Teaching.* Reston Va.: Association of Teacher Educators.

Dewey, J. (1933) 'Why reflective thinking must have an educational aim', in Archambault, R. (ed.) (1964) *John Dewey on Education: Selected Writings.* Chicago: University of Chicago Press.

Kolb, D. and Fry, R. (1975) 'Toward an applied theory of experiential learning', in Cooper, C. (ed.) *Theories of Group Processes*, 33–4. London: Wiley.

Schön, D. (1983) *The Reflective Practitioner.* New York: Basic Books.

Schön, D. (1987) *Educating the Reflective Practitioner.* San Francisco: Jossey-Bass.

Zeichner, K. and Liston, D. (1987) 'Teaching student teachers to reflect', *Harvard Educational Review* **57**(1), 23–48.

Index